A CHOICE OF
ROBERT SOUTHEY'S VERSE

also selected by Geoffrey Grigson

A CHOICE OF WILLIAM MORRIS'S VERSE

A CHOICE OF ROBERT SOUTHEY'S VERSE .

selected
with an introduction by
GEOFFREY GRIGSON

FABER AND FABER

London

First published in 1970
by Faber and Faber Limited
24 Russell Square London WC1
Printed in Great Britain by
Latimer Trend & Co Ltd Plymouth
All rights reserved

ISBN (hard bound edition) 0 571 09055 9
ISBN (edition in paper covers) 0 571 09056 7

Contents

Robert Southey

Born Wine Street, Bristol, 12 August, 1774. Lived with his aunt Elizabeth Tyler, near Bath, 1776–80. Returns home, and is sent away again to a boarding school, 1781. Westminster School, 1788 to 1792, when he is expelled for a school magazine article in which he wrote that flogging performed the will of Satan. Balliol College, Oxford, 1793–4, at this time a Jacobin in sympathy with the French Revolution. Meets Coleridge, two years his junior, 1794, and formulates his plan of Pantisocracy: the foundation of an ideal farming community in America. *Poems by Robert Lovell and Robert Southey,* 1794 (dated 1795). Marries Edith Fricker, 1795. In Portugal, 1795–6. *Poems,* 1797–9. Verses parodied in the *Anti-Jacobin,* 1797. First meeting with Wordsworth, 1798. Lives at Westbury-on-Trym, where he writes all the best of his shorter poems, 1798–9. *Thalaba the Destroyer,* 1801. Visits Coleridge at Greta Hall, Keswick, 1803, Greta Hall becoming his home for life. Coleridge in his notebook records his character of 'Australis', 1804. *Madoc,* and *Metrical Tales,* 1805. Meets Walter Savage Landor, 1808. *Curse of Kehama,* 1810. Meets Shelley, 1811. Made Poet Laureate, meets Byron, publishes *Life of Nelson,* 1813. *Roderick,* 1814. Byron writes a satirical dedication of *Don Juan* to Southey, 1818 (this dedication, which also attacked Coleridge and Wordsworth, not printed until 1833). *Life of Wesley,* 1820. *A Vision of Judgement,* 1821. Byron, in his own *Vision of Judgement,* blisteringly ridicules Southey, his politics and his writing, 1822. Publishes first two of seven volumes of *The Doctor,* 1834. His wife goes mad 1834; and dies 1837. *Collected Poems,* 1837–8. Marries Caroline Bowles, 1839. After some years of mental decay, dies at Greta Hall, March 21, 1843, aged sixty-nine, and is buried in Crosthwaite churchyard.

7

The text of the poems, except 'The Devil's Thoughts' and 'Inscription for a Coffee Pot' (J. W. Warter's *Selections from the Letters of Robert Southey*, 1856, vol. iv, pp. 203–4) is taken from *The Poetical Works of Robert Southey, Collected by Himself*, 1837–8.

The dates and places following each poem are from *Poetical Works*, unless in brackets. Titles which are not Southey's are in brackets. So are editorial notes.

Introduction

In his special way a delightful poet, Southey carries a most peculiar load of posthumous disadvantage. He is not allowed to stand on his own legs, by himself. He is for ever associated with Wordsworth, even more with Coleridge, who was his brother-in-law. So his character must always be compared with the characters of those great men, his poems must always be in the shadow of their great poems, it must be remembered always that he reviewed *Lyrical Ballads* and dismissed 'The Ancient Mariner' as 'a Dutch attempt at German sublimity'. His 'political apostasy', too,—his move from left to right—is always liable to be spoken of as worse or more blameworthy than the same transition in other people; in Wordsworth, for example.

Still, there are advantages in this disadvantage. Coleridge, a uniquely shrewd psychologist, knew Southey intimately. He was attracted by him, and repelled by him. He knew his merits and demerits both as a man and as a writer, and he was not backward in recording his judgement. Smarting a little under Southey's goodness, generosity, and reliability, and never quite forgetting that dismissal of his 'Ancient Mariner', the notes he left explain both Southey and his better poems.

They are the light poems from the surface layer of a poet, who, as Coleridge said, was in prose a master of English almost without fault. The depth of Southey—if there was a depth—remained inaccessible to himself.

If this sounds too solemn for the writer of Bishop Hatto and the rats or of the Pindaric ode on Gooseberry-Pie, let us postpone Coleridge on the character and works of 'Australis', and revert to Southey's account, at once pleasing and intimidating, of his own unusual childhood. He was born in Bristol on August 12th, 1774, the eldest surviving child of a young, not

9

very well educated or at all bookish draper and his wife. Instead of being allowed to enjoy a normal steadiness of love, Robert Southey was handed over by his parents to an aunt, who lived on the outskirts of Bath, a few miles away. The young draper was neither, one supposes, too secure nor too successful, his wife was timid, and this aunt of Southey's, her half-sister, many years older, was masterful and by comparison well-to-do, at all events independent; a middle-aging beauty who had never married.

From two until he was six, it was this bizarre imperious woman Southey had to endure, her household, her friends, her temper. She lived in a mixture of elegance and penury; she dressed up for outings and slopped around at home in old clothes and an old bedgown. In her nicely furnished drawing-room a curtain kept flies and sunshine from one of the two portraits Gainsborough had painted of her. She suffered from ideas—that poor-house inmates (a French idea) should sleep on mattresses stuffed with beech leaves, that her small nephew—though nothing came of it—should be educated (France again) on the principles of Rousseau. What the small nephew most remembered, within the walls of her house, was inaction and boredom and having to sleep in her bed and not move in the mornings until she was ready to get up—late; also her excessive hatred of dust and dirt. 'She had a cup once buried for six weeks, to purify it from the lips of one whom she accounted unclean'; and the child was not allowed to do anything—such as play in the garden—which might dirty him. He sat too often and too long in decorous immobility. Years afterwards Southey recalled an early dream which illustrates this alienated time in his life: he dreamt that he was in the house of a great friend of his aunt's, whom she dominated no less than she dominated Southey's mother. The Devil was coming to honour this Miss Palmer (whose father owned the theatre in Bath) with a morning visit. Small Southey sat there trembling 'on one of the flat-bottomed mahogany chairs', while Miss Palmer was 'bustling about in all the hurry and delight of receiving unexpectedly a visit from a great person.' ' "Be seated, dear Mr. Devil." ' Southey recalled Miss Palmer's smile and the Devil's smirk. 'The villainous nose and eyes of old Horny, and his diabolical tail, are before my eyes at this moment'—which suggests an infancy punished or controlled with threats of what the devil might do to small boys who failed to behave. More to the point is that this great recorder of his dreams (which were often morbid, and to do with death and decay—of being clasped by a skeleton, of the dust of the dead resembling damp snuff, or the dead smelling like 'the bitter pungency of cheese in its blackest state of putrefaction') should so often have dreamt about the mother he had been deprived of in those infant years—and, at that, not once but twice; since, having been restored to his mother after four years of dictatorial and eccentric Aunt Tyler, he soon lost her again by being sent off to a boarding school outside Bristol. His mother was to die in 1802. Two years after her death he recorded his long habit of kissing her and weeping on her in his dreams. She came into his dreams, 'her perfect image living before me,' but his dream-feeling each time was one of sorrow.

The child had been driven in upon himself. A hard protective cuticle had grown over his emotive centre; and he had survived, at a price.

There is no need to follow Southey through the detail of his unfolding life, Westminster, Oxford, early association and walking tours with Coleridge, the plans of Pantisocracy, of an ideal community in America, and then the steady career, the long residence in the Lakes at Greta Hall. Because of Coleridge, and of Byron, much of all this is among the common knowledge of literary biography. One might, though, before coming back to Coleridge and Southey in conjunction, indulge a word on that fatal family of three sisters, Edith, Sarah and Mary Fricker, of Bristol, needlework girls, three of the five daughters of a failed and dead manufacturer of sugar-boiling pans, Pantisocratic wives-to-be of three intending Pantisocrats, Southey, Coleridge, and Robert Lovell, minor poet who died young, and soon, in 1796: three girls of attractive looks and bodies, but, as was to be shown before long, decidedly sparse and unattractive minds. Edith Fricker, Edith Southey, was to be described by her Coleridge niece as having been 'an exceedingly fine girl but very inanimate'.[1] Southey, one supposes, could be held responsible for the mis-mating of Coleridge, uniquely born to love, with Sarah Fricker, unremarkably born to be shrill, mindless, and irritating. At any rate it was Southey who introduced them; and brought Coleridge near to the decision, if not to the boil. These three graces of the ordinary Coleridge himself, in his heart, perhaps blamed on the too blameless Southey; and it may wryly be recalled that Southey—after Coleridge parted from Sarah—had them to himself, all three—his inanimate Edith, widow Lovell, and Sarah, with 'her inveterate habits of puny thwarting and un-remitting dyspathy', as her husband said—for long years, in Greta Hall.

The character presented by the ever hard-working, ever equable supporter of wife, children, sisters-in-law, and Coleridge's children as well, was one of a righteousness hard to assail, even if this equable man was also self-righteous. The trouble was to find his heart; to find what Southey was, in fact.

It was in 1803, some years before all such duties and res-ponsibilities devolved on him, that Southey and his wife and their first child had come north to Keswick, to Coleridge's home at Greta Hall, bringing with them Mary Fricker—Mary Lovell. They arrived in September. Sixteen months later Coleridge, ill at the Wordsworth's home at Grasmere but enjoying a rest from all the trio of Frickers, and from Southey too, put down a note, as if thinking of the sisters, about the moralistic flowers of female conversation marked by 'dimness of mind' and ruthless application of the moral Rule of Three, by which all things were solved and ordered; and then turned, in his next entry, to consider the character of 'Australis', of Southey, his good brother-in-law, as 'a striking illustration of the Basis of Morals'. Coleridge was now in his thirty-first, Southey in his thirtieth year.

[1] Imperious Aunt Tyler at once dropped her nephew when she learnt of the Pantisocratic plan and his engagement to dim and penniless Miss Fricker, turning him out of doors, at Bristol where she was then living, at night, into the rain. She allowed herself no recon-ciliation.

First the credit side of this man he had liked, disliked, separated from, and joined again:

With truth, & with the warm colouring of one who feels the Truth, detail his Life, as a History, & the Tenor of his Life, as a system of Habits of his never once stumbling Temperance, his unstained Chastity from his Infancy to the present Hour, . . . the simplicity of his daily Life, the Industry, & vigorous Perseverance in his Pursuit, the worthiness & dignity of these Pursuits, his Liberality & fatherly conduct to his Brothers & Relatives—& for their sake how he submits to *review & Job*, yet by unexampled Industry can do this & yet do more than almost any other man, in the Subjects of his Choice & Ambition/his punctuality in all things—he inflicts none of those small Pains & Discomforts, which your irregular men scatter about them, & vice versâ, bestows all the pleasures which regular correspondence, & a *reliability* in all things great & small can give/—he is kind to his servants, & he is more than kind—he is *good* to them/ Bella[1] for instance/—all his works subserve Humanity, & the great cause of Peace, Equality, & pure Religion—and above all, of domestic Fidelity & Attachments of which as a Husband (& no doubt, he will as a Father) he is himself in his real Life a Pattern in the eyes of ordinary good men/ —All this Australis *does*, & if all Goodness consists in definite, observable, & rememberable *Actions*, Australis is only not perfect, his good Actions so many, his unad[mirable] ones so few, & (with one or two exceptions) so venial.

Then—the other side of virtue:

But now what is Australis? I can tell you, what he is NOT. He is not a man of warmth, or delicacy of Feeling, HE IS NOT self-oblivious or self-diffused, or acquainted with his own nature: & when warped by Resentment or Hatred, not incapable of doing base actions, at all events most *very*, or *damn'd*, indelicate actions, without hesitation at the moment, or any after- remorse.

And then, as if giving expression to truths which oughtn't

[1] Bella was Southey's widowed sister-in-law, Mary Lovell.

really to be expressed, Coleridge continued in a Latin paren-
thesis to recall that review of *Lyrical Ballads*, six years before
(one does not forget such things), as well as snide remarks
directed against himself, and angry charges that he had been
ungrateful, and sneers at Sarah, whom Australis had called that
'Meek Sister in the Family of Christ', and small and large
poetic thefts, and something unbecoming and insufficiently
decorous about Southey, the result, he continues in English, of
'an unfathoming (and not only self-unfathomed, but even
self-unsounded) Spirit—'

> The smiles, the emanations, the perpetual Sea-like Sound
> & Motion of Virtuousness, which is Love, is wanting—/
> He is a clear handsome piece of Water in a Park, moved
> from without—or at best, a smooth stream with one
> current, & tideless, & of which you can only avail yourself
> to one purpose.

'A clear handsome piece of water in a Park'—one remembers
other slightly exasperated comments Southey had wrung or
was to wring from Coleridge, who wavered in his estimate of
Southey as a poet; remarks that Southey was 'a Salmon
dressed with Shrimp Sauce', that 'the enthusiasm of friend-
ship' wasn't with Southey and himself, that reconciled or no,
they had become 'acquaintances', without mutual esteem or
love, that Southey was scarcely a poet, and that 'the very word
metaphysics' was an abomination to him.

Having both the huge poems and the poet in mind, Byron
wasn't so far wrong when he wrote with such sharp fun in *his*
'Vision of Judgment' of St. Peter knocking Southey into his
lake, where

> He first sank to the bottom—like his works,
> But soon rose to the surface—like himself.

In a clear handsome piece of water, situated in a park, there
are no metaphysics; there is no depth, the bottom is visible;
and the poems of such a man are likely to be what in fact
Southey's poems are, whether the shorter ones, delightful in his
special way, or the long and really tedious and nearly lifeless
moral epics I have not represented—save for one short piece—

14

in this selection. Coleridge's private image for Southey may
have been correct, or he might more fairly have urged that it
was impossible to reach a heart so overlaid. Either way the
trouble, the explanation was surely that early childhood, not
once, but twice torn out of the bosom of motherhood, that
early expulsion into the unwanted bed and the unwanted draw-
ing-room of Miss Tyler of Bath. But then not all good poems
are deep ones, or great ones, and one element in the way
Southey's better poems are delightful is akin to an element not
so far mentioned in his character.

Like many men or women whose centre one cannot reach, if
centre they have, Southey could be gay on the surface, charm-
ingly inconsequent, and full of nonsense; though an inch
deeper one found rectitude, it seems, but not tenderness, or
warmth, or that 'perpetual Sea-like Sound and Motion of
Virtuousness, which is Love.' He could make light poems
marked by that same nonsense, that same most engaging
nonsense, touched as the poems might be with sententiousness
or moral irony. Or, the other way round, a sententious or
moral piece or a scrap of pedantry might succeed by its flavour
of nonsense, by the presence of the poet's tongue in his cheek.
If Southey could easily be parodied, one feels, in poem after
poem, even poems mainly serious, that he stations himself de-
liberately on the verge of self-parody, in rhythm and movement
and in statement (isn't Southey's tongue in his cheek, for in-
stance, in 'The Old Man's Comforts'—'You are old, Father
William', page 74, or in the dactylics of 'The Soldier's Wife',
page 24, or the sapphics of 'The Widow', page 25—

Cold was the night wind, drifting fast the snow fell

—parodied to such effect in the *Anti-Jacobin*?). Coupled with
self-parody a clever touch of the morbid recalls to us both his
dreams and the fear induced in him during childhood perhaps
by threats and certainly by the stories mentioned in his auto-
biographical letters, which were more than he could bear.
Bishop Hatto is eaten by rats (which are not the pantomime
rats of 'The Pied Piper'), Bishop Bruno's hand is taken by death:

His cheek grows pale, and his eye-balls glare
And stiff round his tonsure bristled his hair;
With that there came one from the masquers' band,
And took the Bishop by the hand.

The bony hand suspended his breath,
His marrow grew cold at the touch of Death;
On saints in vain he attempted to call,
Bishop Bruno fell dead in the palace hall.

But the Southey who remembers, the Southey who dreams and
half fools with the rotting dead and the skeleton and the skull,
is the Southey who also writes to his friend Grosvenor Bedford
about gooseberries and pies: 'Two gooseberry pies being sup-
posed, their paste made at the same time, and indeed of one
mass, the gooseberries gathered from the same bushes and of
equal age, the sugar in just proportion, and clouted cream to
eat with both, it follows that the largest is preferable. I love
gooseberry pie, Grosvenor; and I think the case is plain' (see the
poem on page 82); this Southey of the dust of death like
damp stuff is also the Southey who describes himself as Robert
the Rhymer, aged 55, singing like a lark in the morning and
nightingalizing in the evening, 'warbling house-notes wild':

His voice is as good as when he was young,
And he has teeth enough left to keep-in his tongue.
A man he is by nature merry,
Somewhat Tom-foolish, and comical, very

Coleridge remarked that the poems of Crabbe (which he did
not much care for) were founded on observation and real life,
whereas Southey's were founded on books and fancy. He also
spoke of not wishing to compose 'with the facility of appro-
priation from the books and the conversation of others that
Southey possesses,' he talked of Southey the poet as a 'jewel-
setter': 'whatever he read he instantly applied to the formation
or adorning of a story'. So it is that Southey makes ridiculous
fun in 'The Amatory Poems of Abel Shufflebottom' (pages
66-73) of the nonsense of the magazine versifiers of his day,

so Bishop Hatto's ballad (page 60) is made to hang on an account of the Bishop which Southey had read in *Coryat's Crudities*, so 'Bishop Bruno' (page 40) grows from a few sentences encountered in Heywood's *Hierarchie of the Blessed Angels*, as Southey, curious reader, burrows his indefatigable omnivorous way through the peculiarities of literature.

Yet his poems and himself—the self of 'Australis'—and the history of his life are related. Southey wrote many of his best poems in one brief period, long before he drudged to the last line of the last of those epical romances which do so much resemble pictures by John Martin turned back into literature, and long before he was made a safe and respectable Poet Laureate, in 1813, as second choice to Walter Scott. Under these poems will be found the word Westbury and the year 1798 or 1799. In June 1798, he set up home, independently, for the first time, with his young inanimate wife Edith, and not only with his wife, but with his mother at last (who had now been a widow for some five years). He had found and rented a former ale-house at Westbury-on-Trym, today a Bristol suburb, then a Gloucestershire village, on a small stream running quickly down into the tidal Avon. Painted, papered and repaired, and with plenty of room, a garden well-stocked, and pleasant views, this house was further blest with housemartins nesting under the eaves. Having no name, the Southeys named it Martin Hall. 'We christened the house properly, I assure you,' Southey wrote to his brother, 'as the martins have colonized all round it, and doubly lucky must the house be on which they so build and bemire. We hesitated between the appropriate names of Rat Hall, Mouse Mansion, Vermin Villa, Cockroach Castle, Cobweb Cottage, and Spider Lodge; but as we routed out the spiders,'—see the spider poem on page 28 —'stopped the rat holes, and found no cockroaches, we bethought of the animals without, and dubbed it Martin Hall.' They picked red or black currants in the garden, and lived 'upon currant puddings'. 'We have bespoke a cat, a great carroty cat.'

The tone of the letters is the tone of several of the poems, Southey contented, Southey fooling, and with sympathy to spare. The winter at Westbury-on-Trym was sharp, but what of bad weather or cold feet, in this twenty-fourth and twenty-fifth year of Southey's life, the first perfect year, perhaps, of recovered and repaired childhood, the first year of the domesticity which the lack of domesticity in that broken childhood always compelled him to value so highly?[1]

'We are enduring something like a Kamtschatkan winter here. I am obliged to take my daily walk, and, though I go wrapped up in my greatcoat, almost like a dancing bear in hirsute appearance, still the wind pierces me.' That was in December 1798. Then in January: 'The frost stopped the pump and the press. . . .Our bread has been so hard, that no one in the house except myself could cut it, and it made my arm ache for the whole day.'

But he saw the martins again around Martin Hall, and to the Westbury poems of 1798—'A Spider', 'The Cross Roads', 'The Witch', 'The Old Mansion-House', 'The Surgeon's Warning', 'The Battle of Blenheim', 'The Holly Tree' and 'Bishop Bruno'—he added in 1799 (before midsummer, when he was compelled for some reason or other to abandon Martin Hall) his masterpiece, 'God's Judgement on a Wicked Bishop' (Bishop Hatto), as well as 'The Old Man's Comforts' (Father William), 'To a Bee', 'The Ebb Tide', 'The Pig', the sonnets to the winter and to the delaying spring, the sonnet of farewell and the last at any rate of his Shufflebottom parodies. The Westbury poems of 1788 and 1789, the poems of a twelve-month, many of them of considerable length, include more than forty others which I have not reprinted in this selection—altogether a quite extraordinary crop for so short a time, even allowing for Southey's having undertaken to write poems for the *Morning Post*, in which most of these Westbury poems

---

[1] In his 'Hymn to the Penates' of 1796, Southey recalled the grief and shock of leaving home, the second time, for his boarding school—

> And the first painful smile that clothed my front
> With feelings not its own.

He wrote of how lights coming from some lonely house told his heart, later on, when he was homeless, of the joy of home.

appeared, at a guinea a week; allowing also for their light manner, and for the fact that they were not all of his most successful. 'This was one of the happiest portions of my life', he wrote afterwards, in 1837, and happiness was at least half the explanation: 'I never before or since produced so much poetry in the same space of time.'

Indeed in the forty years from the day when he came to rest in Greta Hall in 1803 until his death there in 1843, he was to write, among much verse, only a few more poems of engaging quality, all of them—like the 'Proem' to 'The Poet's Pilgrimage', a long piece of 1816, about the Laureate's correct visit to the battlefield of Waterloo—grounded on the continued pleasures of having a home and children.

A few of Southey's poems—very few—emerge from Southey *vis-à-vis* nature. This seems curious. In childhood he had been a hunter after flowers and insects. He likes to tell us of his sensitivity to the evocative scent of garden flowers—almost boasting, in his autobiographical letters, that unlike himself, Wordsworth had no sense of smell (though on one occasion, he says, the faculty operated, and Wordsworth smelt a bed of stocks in flower, the scent coming to him 'like a vision of Paradise'). In his letters and his prose, too, he often recorded immediate fresh response, for example to scenery; yet as if the scene were strictly no more than transient and external. One is back at the question of Southey and metaphysics. Wherever Southey's conventional deity was located, it was altogether above and outside phenomena; for him, no very concrete immanence, none of the pantheistic leanings, or temptations, of Wordsworth; no Coleridgean search for unity in multaneity: for him, the clear water in the park, little even of what Henry James was to call 'the happy mean between the sensible and the metaphysical'; for him, in his poems, little, either, except indirectly or lightly, of himself—'I have a dislike to all strong emotion'; and only a modicum of his own feelings—'My opinions are for the world, but my feelings are to myself.' No lyric subjectivity. No lyricism.

Wordsworth is reported as saying after his death that the

'Stanzas' ('My days among the Dead are past') were a 'true and touching representation' of Southey's character: the Dead in that poem (page 104) being the dead in the 14,000 books of Southey's library, from the windows of which he looked out to Derwentwater, Bassenthwaite and the mountains. Only with the dead, with books, can such a 'clear' character as Southey converse, much as a king or queen, it is said, can converse only with horses; with himself, in a deep degree, with others of the living in a deep degree, Southey was unable to talk; and standing by temperament outside the tradition which stretches from Vaughan to Hardy, or, accented a little differently, from Ronsard to Victor Hugo, he could scarcely hold a profound dialogue with the lakes, and the mountains beyond the lakes, or the honeysuckle scent by the water, or the parsley-fern on the rock. It is recorded of him that in his dotage he could only sit and pat his books affectionately with both hands. But he is far from the only poet whose bookish poems are agreeable—bookish poems, in his case, in an English, at its best, like the English of his prose, 'next door to faultless' and tinged so often or spiced with his agreeable (again bookish) morbidity. I have no wish to be apologizing for Southey—or Southey's poems; but we should more often than we do—especially now, in a time of existentialist or confessional absolutism or conceit—remember his friend Coleridge decrying the application to poems of an Act of Uniformity.

GEOFFREY GRIGSON

Installation at Oxford. 1793.

Toll on, toll on, old Bell! I'll neither pass
The cold and weary hour in heartless rites.
Nor doze away the time. The fire burns bright,
And, bless the maker of this Windsor-Chair!
(Of polish'd cherry, elbow'd, saddle-seated.)
This is the throne of comfort. I will sit
And study here devoutly: . . not my Euclid, . .
For Heaven forbid that I should discompose
That Spider's excellent geometry!
I'll study thee, Puss! Not to make a picture,
I hate your canvass cats and dogs and fools,
Themes that disgrace the pencil. Thou shalt give
A moral subject, Puss. Come, look at me; . .
Lift up thin emerald eyes! Aye, purr away!
For I am praising thee, I tell thee, Puss,
And Cats as well as Kings like flattery.
For three whole days I heard an old Fur-gown
Bepraised, that made a Duke a Chancellor;
Bepraised in prose it was, bepraised in verse:
Lauded in pious Latin to the skies;
Kudos'd egregiously in heathen Greek;
In sapphics sweetly incensed; glorified
In proud alcaics; in hexameters
Applauded to the very Galleries
That did applaud again, whose thunder-claps,
Higher and longer with redoubling peals
Rung, when they heard the illustrious furbelow'd
Heroically in Popean rhyme
Tee-ti-tum'd, in Miltonic blank bemouth'd;
Prose, verse, Greek, Latin, English, rhyme and blank,
Apotheosi-chancellor'd in all,
Till Eulogy, with all her wealth of words,
Grew bankrupt, all-too-prodigal of praise,

And panting Panegyric toil'd in vain
O'er-task'd in keeping pace with such desert.
   Though I can poetize right willingly,
Puss, on thy well-streak'd coat, to that Fur-gown
I was not guilty of a single line:
'Twas an old furbelow, that would hang loose,
And wrap round any one, as it were made
To fit him only, so it were but tied
With a blue ribband.
                     What a power there is
In beauty! Within these forbidden walls
Thou hast thy range at will, and when perchance
The Fellows see thee, Puss, they overlook
Inhibitory laws or haply think
The statute was not made for Cats like thee;
For thou art beautiful as ever Cat
That wantoned in the joy of kittenhood.
Aye, stretch thy claws, thou democratic beast, . .
I like thine independence. Treat thee well,
Thou art as playful as young Innocence;
But if we act the governor, and break
The social compact, Nature gave those claws
And taught thee how to use them. Man, methinks,
Master and slave alike, might learn from thee
A salutary lesson: but the one
Abuses wickedly his power unjust,
The other crouches, spaniel-like, and licks
The hand that strikes him. Wiser animal,
I look at thee, familiarized, yet free;
And, thinking that a child with gentle hand
Leads by a string the large-limb'd Elephant,
With mingled indignation and contempt
Behold his drivers goad the biped beast.

The Chapel Bell

Lo I, the man who from the Muse did ask
    Her deepest notes to swell the Patriot's meeds,
Am now enforced, a far unfitter task,
    For cap and gown to leave my minstrel weeds;
For yon dull tone that tinkles on the air
Bids me lay by the lyre and go to morning prayer.

Oh how I hate the sound! it is the knell
    That still a requiem tolls to Comfort's hour;
And loth am I, at Superstition's bell,
    To quit or Morpheus' or the Muse's bower:
Better to lie and doze, than gape amain,
Hearing still mumbled o'er the same eternal strain.

Thou tedious herald of more tedious prayers,
    Say, dost thou ever summon from his rest
One being wakening to religious cares?
    Or rouse one pious transport in the breast?
Or rather, do not all reluctant creep
To linger out the time in listlessness or sleep?

I love the bell that calls the poor to pray,
    Chiming from village church its cheerful sound,
When the sun smiles on Labour's holy-day,
    And all the rustic train are gather'd round,
Each deftly dizen'd in his Sunday's best,
And pleased to hail the day of piety and rest.

And when, dim shadowing o'er the face of day
    The mantling mists of even-tide rise slow,
As through the forest gloom I wend my way,
    The minster curfew's sullen voice I know,
And pause, and love its solemn toll to hear,
As made by distance soft it dies upon the ear.

Nor with an idle nor unwilling ear
  Do I receive the early passing-bell;
For, sick at heart with many a secret care,
  When I lie listening to the dead man's knell,
I think that in the grave all sorrows cease,
And would full fain recline my head and be at peace.

But thou, memorial of monastic gall!
  What fancy sad or lightsome hast thou given?
Thy vision-scaring sounds alone recall
  The prayer that trembles on a yawn to heaven,
The snuffling, snaffling Fellow's nasal tone,
And Romish rites retain'd, though Romish faith be flown.

Oxford, 1793.

The Soldier's Wife

DACTYLICS.

Weary way-wanderer, languid and sick at heart,
Travelling painfully over the rugged road,
Wild-visaged Wanderer! God help thee wretched one!

Sorely thy little one drags by thee bare-footed,
Cold is the baby that hangs at thy bending back,
Meagre and livid and screaming for misery.

*Woe-begone mother, half anger, half agony,
As over thy shoulder thou lookest to hush the babe,
Bleakly the blinding snow beats in thy hagged face.

Ne'er will thy husband return from the war again,
Cold is thy heart and as frozen as Charity!
Cold are thy children.—Now God be thy comforter!

  Br stol, 1795.

    * This stanza was written by S. T. COLERIDGE.

The Widow

SAPPHICS

Cold was the night wind, drifting fast the snow fell,
Wide were the downs and shelterless and naked,
When a poor Wanderer struggled on her journey,
    Weary and way-sore.

Drear were the downs, more dreary her reflections.
Cold was the night-wind, colder was her bosom:
She had no home, the world was all before her,
    She had no shelter.

Fast o'er the heath a chariot rattled by her,
'Pity me!' feebly cried the lonely wanderer;
'Pity me, strangers! lest with cold and hunger
    Here I should perish.

'Once I had friends,—though now by all forsaken!
Once I had parents,—they are now in Heaven!
I had a home once—I had once a husband—
    Pity me, strangers!

'I had a home once—I had once a husband—
I am a widow, poor and broken-hearted!'
Loud blew the wind, unheard was her complaining,
    On drove the chariot.

Then on the snow she laid her down to rest her;
She heard a horseman, 'Pity me!' she groan'd out;
Loud was the wind, unheard was her complaining,
    On went the horseman.

Worn out with anguish, toil and cold and hunger,
Down sunk the Wanderer, sleep had seized her senses;
There did the traveller find her in the morning;
    God had released her.

Bristol, 1795.

To a Goose

If thou didst feed on western plains of yore;
Or waddle wide with flat and flabby feet
Over some Cambrian mountain's plashy moor;
Or find in farmer's yard a safe retreat
From gipsy thieves, and foxes sly and fleet;
If thy grey quills, by lawyer guided, trace
Deeds big with ruin to some wretched race,
Or love-sick poet's sonnet, sad and sweet,
Wailing the rigour of his lady fair;
Or if, the drudge of housemaid's daily toil,
Cobwebs and dust thy pinions white besoil,
Departed Goose! I neither know nor care.
But this I know, that we pronounced thee fine,
Season'd with sage and onions, and port wine.

London, 1798.

The Complaints of the Poor

And wherefore do the Poor complain?
    The Rich Man ask'd of me; . . .
Come walk abroad with me, I said,
    And I will answer thee.

'Twas evening, and the frozen streets
    Were cheerless to behold,
And we were wrapt and coated well,
    And yet we were a-cold.

26

We met an old bare-headed man,
   His locks were thin and white;
I ask'd him what he did abroad
   In that cold winter's night;

The cold was keen indeed, he said,
   But at home no fire had he,
And therefore he had come abroad
   To ask for charity.

We met a young bare-footed child,
   And she begg'd loud and bold;
I ask'd her what she did abroad
   When the wind it blew so cold;

She said her father was at home,
   And he lay sick a-bed,
And therefore was it she was sent
   Abroad to beg for bread.

We saw a woman sitting down
   Upon a stone to rest,
She had a baby at her back
   And another at her breast;

I ask'd her why she loiter'd there
   When the night-wind was so chill;
She turn'd her head and bade the child
   That scream'd behind, be still;

Then told us that her husband served,
   A soldier, far away,
And therefore to her parish she
   Was begging back her way.

We met a girl, her dress was loose
   And sunken was her eye,
Who with a wanton's hollow voice
   Address'd the passers-by;

I ask'd her what there was in guilt
That could her heart allure
To shame, disease, and late remorse;
She answer'd she was poor.

I turn'd me to the Rich Man then,
For silently stood he, . . .
You ask'd me why the Poor complain,
And these have answer'd thee!

London, 1798.

To a Spider

1

Spider! thou need'st not run in fear about
To shun my curious eyes;
I won't humanely crush thy bowels out
Lest thou should'st eat the flies;
Nor will I roast thee with a damn'd delight
Thy strange instinctive fortitude to see,
For there is One who might
One day roast me.

2

Thou art welcome to a Rhymer sore-perplext,
The subject of his verse;
There's many a one who on a better text
Perhaps might comment worse.
Then shrink not, old Free-Mason, from my view,
But quietly like me spin out the line;
Do thou thy work pursue
As I will mine.

3

Weaver of snares, thou emblemest the ways
Of Satan, Sire of lies;
Hell's huge black Spider, for mankind he lays
His toils, as thou for flies.
When Betty's busy eye runs round the room,
Woe to that nice geometry, if seen!
But where is he whose broom
The earth shall clean?

4

Spider! of old thy flimsy webs were thought,
And 'twas a likeness true,
To emblem laws in which the weak are caught,
But which the strong break through:
And if a victim in thy toils is ta'en,
Like some poor client is that wretched fly;
I'll warrant thee thou'lt drain
His life-blood dry.

5

And is not thy weak work like human schemes
And care on earth employ'd?
Such are young hopes and Love's delightful dreams
So easily destroy'd!
So does the Statesman, whilst the Avengers sleep,
Self-deem'd secure, his wiles in secret lay,
Soon shall destruction sweep
His work away.

6

Thou busy labourer! one resemblance more
May yet the verse prolong,
For, Spider, thou art like the Poet poor,
Whom thou hast help'd in song.

Both busily our needful food to win.
We work, as Nature taught, with ceaseless pains;
        Thy bowels thou dost spin,
            I spin my brains.

Westbury, 1798.

The Holly Tree

1

O Reader! hast thou ever stood to see
        The Holly Tree?
The eye that contemplates it well perceives
        Its glossy leaves
Order'd by an intelligence so wise,
As might confound the Atheist's sophistries.

2

Below, a circling fence, its leaves are seen
        Wrinkled and keen;
No grazing cattle through their prickly round
        Can reach to wound;
But as they grow where nothing is to fear,
Smooth and unarm'd the pointless leaves appear.

3

I love to view these things with curious eyes,
        And moralize:
And in this wisdom of the Holly Tree
        Can emblems see
Wherewith perchance to make a pleasant rhyme,
One which may profit in the after time.

Thus, though abroad perchance I might appear
  Harsh and austere,
To those who on my leisure would intrude
  Reserved and rude,
Gentle at home amid my friends I'd be
Like the high leaves upon the Holly Tree.

And should my youth, as youth is apt I know,
  Some harshness show,
All vain asperities I day by day
  Would wear away,
Till the smooth temper of my age should be
Like the high leaves upon the Holly Tree.

And as when all the summer trees are seen
  So bright and green,
The Holly leaves a sober hue display
  Less bright than they,
But when the bare and wintry woods we see,
What then so cheerful as the Holly Tree?

So serious should my youth appear among
  The thoughtless throng,
So would I seem amid the young and gay
  More grave than they,
That in my age as cheerful I might be
As the green winter of the Holly Tree.

Westbury, 1798.

The Cross Roads

The tragedy related in this Ballad happened about the year
1760, in the parish of Bedminster, near Bristol. One who
was present at the funeral told me the story and the circum-
stances of the interment, as I have versified them.

I

There was an old man breaking stones
    To mend the turnpike way;
He sate him down beside a brook,
And out his bread and cheese he took,
    For now it was mid-day.

2

He leant his back against a post,
    His feet the brook ran by:
And there were water-cresses growing,
And pleasant was the water's flowing,
    For he was hot and dry.

3

A soldier with his knapsack on
    Came travelling o'er the down;
The sun was strong and he was tired;
And he of the old man enquired
    'How far to Bristol town?'

4

'Half an hour's walk for a young man,
    By lanes and fields and stiles;
But you the foot-path do not know,
And if along the road you go
    Why then 'tis three good miles.'

5

The soldier took his knapsack off,
  For he was hot and dry;
And out his bread and cheese he took,
And he sat down beside the brook
  To dine in company.

6

'Old friend! in faith,' the soldier says,
  'I envy you almost;
My shoulders have been sorely prest,
And I should like to sit, and rest
  My back against that post.

7

'In such a sweltering day as this
  A knapsack is the devil;
And if on t'other side I sat,
It would not only spoil our chat,
  But make me seem uncivil.'

8

The old man laugh'd and moved . . . 'I wish
  It were a great-arm'd chair!
But this may help a man at need; . .
And yet it was a cursed deed
  That ever brought it there.

9

'There's a poor girl lies buried here,
  Beneath this very place,
The earth upon her corpse is prest,
This post was driven into her breast,
  And a stone is on her face.'

The soldier had but just leant back,
  And now he half rose up.
'There's sure no harm in dining here,
My friend? and yet, to be sincere,
  I should not like to sup.'

'God rest her! she is still enough
  Who sleeps beneath my feet!'
The old man cried. 'No harm I trow,
She ever did herself, though now
  She lies where four roads meet.

'I have past by about that hour
  When men are not most brave;
It did not make my courage fail,
And I have heard the nightingale
  Sing sweetly on her grave.

'I have past by about that hour
  When ghosts their freedom have;
But here I saw no ghastly sight,
And quietly the glow-worm's light
  Was shining on her grave.

'There's one who like a Christian lies
  Beneath the church-tree's shade;
I'd rather go a long mile round
Than pass at evening through the ground
  Wherein that man is laid.

15

'A decent burial that man had,
  The bell was heard to toll,
When he was laid in holy ground,
But for all the wealth in Bristol town
  I would not be with his soul!

16

'Did'st see a house below the hill
  Which the winds and the rains destroy?
In that farm-house did that man dwell,
And I remember it full well
  When I was a growing boy.

17

'But she was a poor parish girl
  Who came up from the west:
From service hard she ran away,
And at that house in evil day
  Was taken in to rest.

18

'A man of a bad name was he,
  An evil life he led;
Passion made his dark face turn white,
And his grey eyes were large and light,
  And in anger they grew red.

19

'The man was bad, the mother worse,
  Bad fruit of evil stem;
'T would make your hair to stand on end
If I should tell to you, my friend,
  The things that were told of them!

20

'Did'st see an out-house standing by?
   The walls alone remain;
It was a stable then, but now
Its mossy roof has fallen through
   All rotted by the rain.

21

'This poor girl she had served with them
   Some half-a-year or more,
When she was found hung up one day,
Stiff as a corpse and cold as clay,
   Behind that stable door.

22

'It is a wild and lonesome place,
   No hut or house is near;
Should one meet a murderer there alone,
'T were vain to scream, and the dying groan
   Would never reach mortal ear.

23

'And there were strange reports about;
   But still the coroner found
That she by her own hand had died,
And should buried be by the way-side,
   And not in Christian ground.

24

'This was the very place he chose,
   Just where these four roads meet;
And I was one among the throng
That hither follow'd them along,
   I shall never the sight forget!

25

'They carried her upon a board
  In the clothes in which she died;
I saw the cap blown off her head,
Her face was of a dark dark red,
  Her eyes were starting wide:

26

'I think they could not have been closed,
  So widely did they strain.
O Lord, it was a ghastly sight,
And it often made me wake at night,
  When I saw it in dreams again.

27

'They laid her where these four roads meet.
  Here in this very place.
The earth upon her corpse was prest,
This post was driven into her breast,
  And a stone is on her face.'

Westbury, 1798.

The Battle of Blenheim

I

It was a summer evening,
  Old Kaspar's work was done,
And he before his cottage door
  Was sitting in the sun,
And by him sported on the green
His little grandchild Wilhelmine.

37

She saw her brother Peterkin
  Roll something large and round,
Which he beside the rivulet
  In playing there had found;
He came to ask what he had found,
That was so large, and smooth, and round.

3

Old Kaspar took it from the boy,
  Who stood expectant by;
And then the old man shook his head
  And with a natural sigh,
"Tis some poor fellow's skull', said he,
'Who fell in the great victory.

4
'I find them in the garden,
  For there's many here about;
And often when I go to plough,
  The ploughshare turns them out!
For many thousand men', said he,
'Were slain in that great victory.'

5
'Now tell us what 't was all about,'
  Young Peterkin, he cries;
And little Wilhelmine looks up
  With wonder-waiting eyes;
'Now tell us all about the war,
And what they fought each other for.'

6
'It was the English', Kaspar cried,
  'Who put the French to rout;
But what they fought each other for,
  I could not well make out;
But everybody said', quoth he,
'That 't was a famous victory.

7

'My father lived at Blenheim then,
　Yon little stream hard by;
They burnt his dwelling to the ground,
　And he was forced to fly;
So with his wife and child he fled,
Nor had he where to rest his head.

8

'With fire and sword the country round
　Was wasted far and wide,
And many a childing mother then,
　And new-born baby died;
But things like that, you know, must be
At every famous victory.

9

'They say it was a shocking sight
　After the field was won;
For many thousand bodies here
　Lay rotting in the sun;
But things like that, you know, must be
After a famous victory.

10

'Great praise the Duke of Marlbro' won,
　And our good Prince Eugene.'
'Why 't was a very wicked thing!'
　Said little Wilhelmine.
'Nay . . nay . . my little girl', quoth he,
'It was a famous victory.

11

'And everybody praised the Duke
　Who this great fight did win.'
'But what good came of it at last?'
　Quoth little Peterkin.
'Why that I cannot tell,' said he,
'But 't was a famous victory.'

Westbury, 1798.

Bishop Bruno

'Bruno, the Bishop of Herbipolitanum, sailing in the river of Danubius, with Henry the Third, then Emperor, being not far from a place which the Germanes call *Ben Strudel*. or the devouring gulfe, which is neere unto Grinon, a castle in Austria, a spirit was heard clamouring aloud, "Ho, ho, Bishop Bruno, whither art thou travelling? but dispose of thyselfe how thou pleasest, thou shalt be my prey and spoil." At the hearing of these words they were all stupified, and the Bishop with the rest crost and blest themselves. The issue was, that within a short time after, the Bishop, feasting with the Emperor in a castle belonging to the Countess of Esburch, a rafter fell from the roof of the chamber wherein they sate, and strooke him dead at the table.'

HEYWOOD's Hierarchie of the Blessed Angels.

Bishop Bruno awoke in the dead midnight,
And he heard his heart beat loud with affright:
He dreamt he had rung the Palace bell,
And the sound it gave was his passing knell.

Bishop Bruno smiled at his fears so vain,
He turned to sleep and he dreamt again;
He rang at the palace gate once more,
And Death was the Porter that open'd the door.

He started up at the fearful dream,
And he heard at his window the screech-owl scream;
Bishop Bruno slept no more that night, . .
Oh, glad was he when he saw the day-light!

Now he goes forth in proud array,
For he with the Emperor dines to-day;
There was not a Baron in Germany
That went with a nobler train than he.

Before and behind his soldiers ride,
The people throng'd to see their pride;
They bow'd the head, and the knee they bent,
But nobody blest him as he went.

So he went on stately and proud,
When he heard a voice that cried aloud,
'Ho! ho! Bishop Bruno! you travel with glee, . .
But I would have you know, you travel to me!'

Behind and before and on either side,
He look'd, but nobody he espied;
And the Bishop at that grew cold with fear,
For he heard the words distinct and clear.

And when he rang at the Palace bell,
He almost expected to hear his knell;
And when the Porter turn'd the key,
He almost expected Death to see.

But soon the Bishop recover'd his glee,
For the Emperor welcomed him royally;
And now the tables were spread, and there
Were choicest wines and dainty fare.

And now the Bishop had blest the meat,
When a voice was heard as he sat in his seat, . .
'With the Emperor now you are dining with glee,
But know, Bishop Bruno! you sup with me!'

The Bishop then grew pale with affright,
And suddenly lost his appetite;
All the wine and dainty cheer
Could not comfort his heart that was sick with fear.

But by little and little recovered he,
For the wine went flowing merrily,
Till at length he forgot his former dread,
And his cheeks again grew rosy red.

When he sat down to the royal fare
Bishop Bruno was the saddest man there;
But when the masquers enter'd the hall,
He was the merriest man of all.

Then from amid the masquers' crowd
There went a voice hollow and loud, . .
'You have past the day, Bishop Bruno, in glee;
But you must pass the night with me!'

His cheek grows pale, and his eye-balls glare,
And stiff round his tonsure bristled his hair;
With that there came one from the masquers' band,
And took the Bishop by the hand.

The bony hand suspended his breath,
His marrow grew cold at the touch of Death;
On saints in vain he attempted to call,
Bishop Bruno fell dead in the palace hall.

Westbury, 1798.

The Witch

NATHANIEL.

Father! here, father! I have found a horse-shoe!
Faith it was just in time; for t' other night
I laid two straws across at Margery's door,
And ever since I fear'd that she might do me
A mischief for 't. There was the Miller's boy
Who set his dog at that black cat of hers, . .
I met him upon crutches, and he told me
'T was all her evil eye.

FATHER.
'Tis rare good luck!
I would have gladly given a crown for one
If 't would have done as well. But where didst find it?

NATHANIEL.
Down on the common; I was going a-field,
And neighbour Saunders pass'd me on his mare;
He had hardly said 'Good day,' before I saw
The shoe drop off. 'T was just upon my tongue
To call him back; . . it makes no difference does it,
Because I know whose 't was?

FATHER.
Why no, it can't.
The shoe's the same, you know; and you did find it.

NATHANIEL.
That mare of his has got a plaguey road
To travel, father; . . and if he should lame her, . .
For she is but tender-footed, . . .

FATHER.
Ay, indeed! . .
I should not like to see her limping back,
Poor beast! . . But charity begins at home,
And, Nat, there's our own horse in such a way
This morning!

NATHANIEL.
Why he han't been rid again!
Last night I hung a pebble by the manger
With a hole through, and everybody says
That 't is a special charm against the hags.

FATHER.

It could not be a proper natural hole then,
Or 't was not a right pebble; . . for I found him
Smoking with sweat, quaking in every limb,
And panting so! Lord knows where he had been
When we were all asleep, through bush and brake,
Up-hill and down-hill all alike, full stretch
At such a deadly rate! . .

NATHANIEL.

By land and water,
Over the sea, perhaps! . . I have heard tell
'T is many thousand miles off at the end
Of the world, where witches go to meet the Devil.
They used to ride on broomsticks, and to smear
Some ointment over them, and then away
Out at the window! but 't is worse than all
To worry the poor beasts so. Shame upon it
That in a Christian country they should let
Such creatures live!

FATHER.

And when there's such plain proof!
I did but threaten her because she robb'd
Our hedge, and the next night there came a wind
That made me shake to hear it in my bed.
How came it that that storm unroof'd my barn,
And only mine in the parish? . . Look at her,
And that's enough; she has it in her face! . .
A pair of large dead eyes, sunk in her head,
Just like a corpse, and pursed with wrinkles round;
A nose and chin that scarce leave room between
For her lean fingers to squeeze in the snuff;
And when she speaks! I'd sooner hear a raven
Croak at my door! . . She sits there, nose and knees,
Smoke-dried and shrivell'd over a starved fire,
With that black cat beside her, whose great eyes
Shine like old Beelzebub's; and to be sure
It must be one of his imps! . . Ay, nail it hard.

44

NATHANIEL.

I wish old Margery heard the hammer go!
She'd curse the music!

FATHER.

              Here's the Curate coming,
He ought to rid the parish of such vermin!
In the old times they used to hunt them out,
And hang them without mercy; but, Lord bless us!
The world is grown so wicked!

CURATE.

              Good day, Farmer!
Nathaniel, what art nailing to the threshold?

NATHANIEL.

A horse-shoe, Sir; 't is good to keep off witchcraft,
And we're afraid of Margery.

CURATE.

              Poor old woman!
What can you fear from her?

FATHER.

              What can we fear?
Who lamed the Miller's boy? who raised the wind
That blew my old barn's roof down? who d' ye think
Rides my poor horse a' nights? who mocks the hounds?
But let me catch her at that trick again,
And I've a silver bullet ready for her,
One that shall lame her, double how she will.

NATHANIEL.

What makes her sit there moping by herself,
With no soul near her but that great black cat?
And do but look at her!

CURATE.
                              Poor wretch; half blind
And crooked with her years, without a child
Or friend in her old age, 't is hard indeed
To have her very miseries made her crimes!
I met her but last week in that hard frost
Which made my young limbs ache, and when I ask'd
What brought her out in the snow, the poor old woman
Told me that she was forced to crawl abroad
And pick the hedges, just to keep herself
From perishing with cold, . . because no neighbour
Had pity on her age; and then she cried,
And said the children pelted her with snow-balls,
And wish'd that she were dead.

FATHER.
                              I wish she was!
She has plagued the parish long enough!

CURATE.
                              Shame, Farmer!
Is that the charity your Bible teaches?

FATHER.
My Bible does not teach me to love witches.
I know what's charity; who pays his tithes
And poor-rates readier?

CURATE.
                              Who can better do it?
You've been a prudent and industrious man,
And God has blest your labour.

FATHER.
                              Why, thank God, Sir,
I've had no reason to complain of fortune.

CURATE.

Complain? why you are wealthy! All the parish
Look up to you.

FATHER.

Perhaps, Sir, I could tell
Guinea for guinea with the warmest of them.

CURATE.

You can afford a little to the poor;
And then, what's better still, you have the heart
To give from your abundance.

FATHER.

God forbid
I should want charity!

CURATE.

Oh! 't is a comfort
To think at last of riches well employ'd!
I have been by a death-bed, and know the worth
Of a good deed at that most aweful hour
When riches profit not.

Farmer, I'm going
To visit Margery. She is sick, I hear; . .
Old, poor and sick! a miserable lot,
And death will be a blessing. You might send her
Some little matter, something comfortable.
That she may go down easier to the grave,
And bless you when she dies.

FATHER.

What! is she going?
Well God forgive her then, if she has dealt
In the black art! I'll tell my dame of it,
And she shall send her something.

47

CURATE.

So I'll say;
And take my thanks for hers.   [*Goes.*]

FATHER.

That's a good man
That Curate, Nat, of ours, to go and visit
The poor in sickness; but he don't believe
In witchcraft, and that is not like a Christian.

NATHANIEL.
And so old Margery's dying!

FATHER.

But you know
She may recover: so drive 't other nail in.

Westbury, 1798.

The Old Mansion-House

STRANGER.

Old friend! why you seem bent on parish duty,
Breaking the highway stones, . . and 't is a task
Somewhat too hard methinks for age like yours!

OLD MAN.
Why yes! for one with such a weight of years
Upon his back! . . I've lived here, man and boy,
In this same parish, well nigh the full age
Of man, being hard upon threescore and ten.
I can remember sixty years ago
The beautifying of this mansion here,
When my late Lady's father, the old Squire,
Came to the estate.

48

STRANGER.

Why then you have outlasted
All his improvements, for you see they're making
Great alterations here.

OLD MAN.

Aye . . great indeed!
And if my poor old Lady could rise up . .
God rest her soul! 't would grieve her to behold
What wicked work is here.

STRANGER.

They've set about it
In right good earnest. All the front is gone;
Here's to be turf, they tell me, and a road
Round to the door. There were some yew trees too
Stood in the court. . .

OLD MAN.

Aye, Master! fine old trees!
Lord bless us! I have heard my father say
His grandfather could just remember back
When they were planted there. It was my task
To keep them trimm'd, and 't was a pleasure to me;
All straight and smooth, and like a great green wall!
My poor old lady many a time would come
And tell me where to clip, for she had play'd
In childhood under them, and 't was her pride
To keep them in their beauty. Plague, I say,
On their new-fangled whimsies! we shall have
A modern shrubbery here stuck full of firs
And your pert poplar trees; . . . I could as soon
Have plough'd my father's grave as cut them down!

STRANGER.

But 't will be lighter and more chearful now;
A fine smooth turf, and with a carriage road
That sweeps conveniently from gate to gate.
I like a shubbery too, for it looks fresh;

And then there's some variety about it.
In spring the lilac and the snow-ball flower,
And the laburnum with its golden strings
Waving in the wind: And when the autumn comes
The bright red berries of the mountain-ash,
With pines enough in winter to look green,
And show that something lives. Sure this is better
Than a great hedge of yew, making it look
All the year round like winter, and for ever
Dropping its poisonous leaves from the under boughs
Wither'd and bare.

OLD MAN.

                Aye! so the new Squire thinks;
And pretty work he makes of it! What 't is
To have a stranger come to an old house!

STRANGER.
It seems you know him not?

OLD MAN.

                   No, Sir, not I.
They tell me he's expected daily now;
But in my Lady's time he never came
But once, for they were very distant kin.
If he had play'd about here when a child
In that forecourt, and eat the yew-berries,
And sate in the porch, threading the jessamine flowers
Which fell so thick, he had not had the heart
To mar all thus!

STRANGER.
            Come ! come ! all is not wrong;
Those old dark windows. . .

OLD MAN.

               They're demolish'd too, . .
As if he could see through casement glass!
The very red-breasts, that so regular
Came to my Lady for her morning crumbs,
Wo'n't know the windows now!

STRANGER.

                  Nay they were small,
And then so darken'd round with jessamine,
Harbouring the vermin; . . yet I could have wish'd
That jessamine had been saved, which canopied
And bower'd and lined the porch.

OLD MAN.

                    It did one good
To pass within ten yards when 't was in blossom.
There was a sweet-briar too that grew beside;
My Lady loved at evening to sit there
And knit; and her old dog lay at her feet
And slept in the sun; 't was an old favourite dog, . .
She did not love him less that he was old
And feeble, and he always had a place
By the fireside: and when he died at last
She made me dig a grave in the garden for him.
For she was good to all! a woeful day
'T was for the poor when to her grave she went!

STRANGER.
They lost a friend then?

OLD MAN.

               You're a stranger here,
Or you wouldn't ask that question. Were they sick?
She had rare cordial waters, and for herbs
She could have taught the Doctors. Then at winter.
When weekly she distributed the bread
In the poor old porch, to see her and to hear

The blessings on her! and I warrant them
There were a blessing to her when her wealth
Had been no comfort else. At Christmas, Sir!
It would have warm'd your heart if you had seen
Her Christmas kitchen, . . how the blazing fire
Made her fine pewter shine, and holly boughs
So chearful red, . . and as for misseltoe, . .
The finest bush that grew in the country round
Was mark'd for Madam. Then her old ale went
So bountiful about! a Christmas cask,
And 't was a noble one! . . God help me, Sir!
But I shall never see such days again.

STRANGER.

Things may be better yet than you suppose,
And you should hope the best.

OLD MAN.

                It don't look well, . .
These alterations, Sir! I'm an old man,
And love the good old fashions; we don't find
Old bounty in new houses. They've destroy'd
All that my Lady loved; her favourite walk
Grubb'd up, . . and they do say that the great row
Of elms behind the house, which meet a-top,
They must fall too. Well! well! I did not think
To live to see all this, and 't is perhaps
A comfort I shan't live to see it long.

STRANGER.

But sure all changes are not needs for the worse,
My friend?

OLD MAN.

         May-hap they mayn't, Sir; . . for all that
I like what I've been used to. I remember
All this from a child up, and now to lose it,
'T is losing an old friend. There's nothing left

As 't was; . . I go abroad and only meet
With men whose fathers I remember boys;
The brook that used to run before my door,
That's gone to the great pond; the trees I learnt
To climb are down; and I see nothing now
That tells me of old times, . . except the stones
In the churchyard. You are young, Sir, and I hope
Have many years in store, . . but pray to God
You mayn't be left the last of all your friends.

                    STRANGER.
Well! well! you've one friend more than you're aware of.
If the Squire's taste don't suit with yours, I warrant
That's all you'll quarrel with: walk in and taste
His beer, old friend! and see if your old Lady
E'er broach'd a better cask. You did not know me,
But we're acquainted now. 'T would not be easy
To make you like the outside; but within,
That is not changed, my friend! you'll always find
The same old bounty and old welcome there.

Westbury, 1798.

The Surgeon's Warning

The subject of this parody was suggested by a friend, to whom
    also I am indebted for some of the stanzas.
Respecting the patent coffins herein mentioned, after the man-
    ner of Catholic Poets, who confess the actions they attribute
    to their Saints and Deity to be but fiction, I hereby declare
    that it is by no means my design to depreciate that useful
    invention; and all persons to whom this Ballad shall come
    are requested to take notice, that nothing herein asserted
    concerning the aforesaid coffins is true, except that the
    maker and patentee lives by St. Martin's Lane.

The doctor whisper'd to the Nurse,
  And the Surgeon knew what he said;
And he grew pale at the Doctor's tale,
  And trembled in his sick-bed.

'Now fetch me my brethren, and fetch them with speed,'
  The Surgeon affrighted said;
'The Parson and the Undertaker,
  Let them hasten or I shall be dead.'

The Parson and the Undertaker
  They hastily came complying,
And the Surgeon's Prentices ran up stairs
  When they heard that their Master was dying.

The Prentices all they enter'd the room,
  By one, by two, by three;
With a sly grin came Joseph in,
  First of the company.

The Surgeon swore as they enter'd his door,
  'T was fearful his oaths to hear, . .
'Now send these scoundrels out of my sight,
  I beseech ye, my brethren dear!'

He foam'd at the mouth with the rage he felt,
  And he wrinkled his black eye-brow,
'That rascal Joe would be at me, I know,
  But zounds, let him spare me now!'

Then out they sent the Prentices,
  The fit it left him weak,
He look'd at his brothers with ghastly eyes,
  And faintly struggled to speak.

'All kinds of carcases I have cut up,
  And now my turn will be;
But, brothers, I took care of you,
  So pray take care of me.

'I have made candles of dead men's fat.
    The Sextons have been my slaves,
I have bottled babes unborn, and dried
    Hearts and livers from rifled graves.

'And my Prentices now will surely come
    And carve me bone from bone,
And I who have rifled the dead man's grave
    Shall never have rest in my own.

'Bury me in lead when I am dead,
    My brethren, I entreat,
And see the coffin weigh'd, I beg,
    Lest the plumber should be a cheat.

'And let it be solder'd closely down,
    Strong as strong can be, I implore;
And put it in a patent coffin,
    That I may rise no more.

'If they carry me off in the patent coffin,
    Their labour will be in vain;
Let the Undertaker see it bought of the maker,
    Who lives by St. Martin's Lane.

'And bury me in my brother's church,
    For that will safer be;
And I implore, lock the church door,
    And pray take care of the key.

'And all night long let three stout men
    The vestry watch within;
To each man give a gallon of beer,
    And a keg of Holland's gin;

'Powder and ball and blunderbuss,
    To save me if he can,
And eke five guineas if he shoot
    A Resurrection Man.

'And let them watch me for three weeks,
  My wretched corpse to save;
For then I think that I may stink
  Enough to rest in my grave.'

The Surgeon laid him down in his bed,
  His eyes grew deadly dim,
Short came his breath, and the struggle of death
  Did loosen every limb.

They put him in lead when he was dead,
  And with precaution meet,
First they the leaden coffin weigh,
  Lest the plumber should be a cheat.

They had it solder'd closely down,
  And examin'd it o'er and o'er,
And they put it in a patent coffin
  That he might rise no more.

For to carry him off in a patent coffin,
  Would, they thought, be but labour in vain,
So the Undertaker saw it bought of the maker.
  Who lives by St. Martin's Lane.

In his brother's church they buried him,
  That safer he might be;
They lock'd the door, and would not trust
  The Sexton with the key.

And three men in the vestry watch
  To save him if they can,
And should he come there to shoot they swear
  A Resurrection Man.

And the first night by lanthorn light
  Through the churchyard as they went,
A guinea of gold the Sexton shew'd
  That Mister Joseph sent.

But conscience was tough, it was not enough,
  And their honesty never swerved,
And they bade him go with Mister Joe
  To the Devil as he deserved.

So all night long by the vestry fire
  They quaff'd their gin and ale,
And they did drink, as you may think,
  And told full many a tale.

The Cock he crew cock-a-doodle-doo,
  Past five! the watchmen said;
And they went away, for while it was day
  They might safely leave the dead.

The second night by lanthorn light
  Through the churchyard as they went,
He whisper'd anew, and shew'd them two
  That Mister Joseph sent.

The guineas were bright and attracted their sight,
  They look'd so heavy and new,
And their fingers itch'd as they were bewitch'd,
  And they knew not what to do.

But they waver'd not long, for conscience was strong
  And they thought they might get more,
And they refused the gold, but not
  So rudely as before.

So all night long by the vestry fire
  They quaff'd their gin and ale,
And they did drink, as you may think,
  And told full many a tale.

The third night as by lantern light
  Through the churchyard they went,
He bade them see, and shew'd them three
  That Mister Joseph sent.

They look'd askaunce with greedy glance,
    The guineas they shone bright,
For the Sexton on the yellow gold
    Let fall his lanthorn light.

And he look'd sly with his roguish eye,
    And gave a well-timed wink,
And they could not stand the sound in his hand,
    For he made the guineas chink.

And conscience, late that had such weight,
    All in a moment fails,
For well they knew that it was true
    A dead man tells no tales.

And they gave all their powder and ball,
    And took the gold so bright,
And they drank their beer and made good cheer
    Till now it was midnight.

Then, though the key of the church door
    Was left with the Parson, his brother,
It open'd at the Sexton's touch, . . .
    Because he had another.

And in they go with that villain Joe,
    To fetch the body by night,
And all the church look'd dismally
    By his dark-lanthorn light.

They laid the pick-axe to the stones,
    And they moved them soon asunder;
They shovell'd away the hard-prest clay,
    And came to the coffin under.

They burst the patent coffin first,
    And they cut through the lead;
And they laugh'd aloud when they saw the shroud,
    Because they had got at the dead.

And they allow'd the Sexton the shroud,
    And they put the coffin back;
And nose and knees they then did squeeze
    The Surgeon in a sack.

The watchmen as they past along
    Full four yards off could smell,
And a curse bestow'd upon the load
    So disagreeable.

So they carried the sack a-pick-a-back,
    And they carved him bone from bone,
But what became of the Surgeon's soul
    Was never to mortal known.

    Westbury, 1796.

(*Sonnet: To Winter*)

A wrinkled, crabbed man they picture thee,
Old Winter, with a rugged beard as grey
As the long moss upon the apple-tree;
Blue-lipt, an ice-drop at thy sharp blue nose,
Close muffled up, and on thy dreary way,
Plodding alone through sleet and drifting snows.
They should have drawn thee by the high-heapt hearth,
Old Winter! seated in the great arm'd chair,
Watching the children at their Christmas mirth;
Or circled by them as thy lips declare
Some merry jest or tale of murder dire,
Or troubled spirit that disturbs the night,
Pausing at times to rouse the mouldering fire,
Or taste the old October* brown and bright.

    Westbury, 1799.

[*i.e. October-brewed ale—'common in the 18th. century', O.E.D.]

(Sonnet: To Spring)

Thou lingerest, Spring! still wintry is the scene,
The fields their dead and sapless russet wear;
Scarce doth the glossy celandine appear
Starring the sunny bank, or early green
The elder yet its circling tufts put forth.
The sparrow tenants still the eaves-built nest
Where we should see our martin's snowy breast
Oft darting out. The blasts from the bleak north
And from the keener east still frequent blow.
Sweet Spring, thou lingerest; and it should be so, .
Late let the fields and gardens blossom out!
Like man when most with smiles thy face is drest,
'Tis to deceive, and he who knows ye best,
When most ye promise, ever most must doubt.

Westbury, 1799.

God's Judgement on a Wicked Bishop

Here followeth the History of HATTO, Archbichop of Mentz.

It hapned in the year 914, that there was an exceeding great
famine in Germany, at what time Otho surnamed the
Great was Emperor, and one Hatto, once Abbot of Fulda,
was Archbishop of Mentz, of the Bishops after Crescens and
Crescentius the two and thirtieth, of the Archbishops after
St. Bonifacius the thirteenth. This Hatto in the time of
this great famine afore-mentioned, when he saw the poor
people of the country exceedingly oppressed with famine,
assembled a great company of them together into a Barne,
and, like a most accursed and mercilesse caitiffe, burnt up
those poor innocent souls, that were so far from doubting
any such matter, that they rather hoped to receive some

60

comfort and relief at his hands. The reason that moved the prelat to commit that execrable impiety was, because he thought the famine would the sooner cease, if those unprofitable beggars that consumed more bread than they were worthy to eat, were dispatched out of the world. For he said that those poor folks were like to Mice, that were good for nothing but to devour corne. But God Almighty, the just avenger of the poor folks' quarrel, did not long suffer this hainous tyranny, this most detestable fact, unpunished. For he mustered up an army of Mice against the Archbishop, and sent them to persecute him as his furious Alastors, so that they afflicted him both day and night, and would not suffer him to take his rest in any place. Whereupon the Prelate, thinking that he should be secure from the injury of Mice if he were in a certain tower, that standeth in the Rhine near to the towne, betook himself unto the said tower as to a safe refuge and sanctuary from his enemies, and locked himself in. But the innumerable troupes of Mice chased him continually very eagerly, and swumme unto him upon the top of the water to execute the just judgement of God, and so at last he was most miserably devoured by those sillie creatures; who pursued him with such bitter hostility, that it is recorded they scraped and knawed out his very name from the walls and tapistry wherein it was written, after they had so cruelly devoured his body. Wherefore the tower wherein he was eaten up by the Mice is shewn to this day, for a perpetual monument to all succeeding ages of the barbarous and inhuman tyranny of this impious Prelate, being situate in a little green Island in the midst of the Rhine near to the towne of Bingen, and is commonly called in the German Tongue the MOWSE-TURN.

CORYAT'S Crudities, pp. 571, 572

Other authors who record this tale say that the Bishop was eaten by Rats.

The summer and autumn had been so wet,
That in winter the corn was growing yet,
'T was a piteous sight to see all around
The grain lie rotting on the ground.

Every day the starving poor
Crowded around Bishop Hatto's door,
For he had a plentiful last-year's store,
And all the neighbourhood could tell
His granaries were furnish'd well.

At last Bishop Hatto appointed a day
To quiet the poor without delay;
He bade them to his great Barn repair,
And they should have food for the winter there.

Rejoiced such tidings good to hear,
The poor folk flock'd from far and near;
The great Barn was full as it could hold
Of women and children, and young and old.

Then when he saw it could hold no more,
Bishop Hatto he made fast the door;
And while for mercy on Christ they call,
He set fire to the Barn and burnt them all.

'I'faith 't is an excellent bonfire!' quoth he,
'And the country is greatly obliged to me,
For ridding it in these times forlorn
Of Rats that only consume the corn.'

So then to his palace returned he,
And he sat down to supper merrily,
And he slept that night like an innocent man;
But Bishop Hatto never slept again.

In the morning as he enter'd the hall
Where his picture hung against the wall,
A sweat like death all over him came,
For the Rats had eaten it out of the frame.

As he look'd there came a man from his farm,
He had a countenance white with alarm;
'My Lord, I open'd your granaries this morn,
And the Rats had eaten all your corn.'

Another came running presently,
And he was pale as pale could be,
'Fly! my Lord Bishop, fly', quoth he,
'Ten thousand Rats are coming this way, . .
The Lord forgive you for yesterday!'

'I'll go to my tower on the Rhine,' replied he,
"'T is the safest place in Germany;
The walls are high and the shores are steep,
And the stream is strong and the water deep.'

Bishop Hatto fearfully hasten'd away,
And he crost the Rhine without delay,
And reach'd his tower, and barr'd with care
All the windows, doors, and loop-holes there.

He laid him down and closed his eyes; . .
But soon a scream made him arise,
He started and saw two eyes of flame
On his pillow from whence the screaming came.

He listen'd and look'd; . . . it was only the Cat;
But the Bishop he grew more fearful for that,
For she sat screaming, mad with fear
At the Army of Rats that were drawing near.

For they have swam over the river so deep,
And they have climb'd the shores so steep,
And up the Tower their way is bent,
To do the work for which they were sent.

They are not to be told by the dozen or score,
By thousands they come, and by myriads and more,
Such numbers had never been heard of before,
Such a judgement had never been witness'd of yore.

Down on his knees the Bishop fell,
And faster and faster his beads did he tell,
As louder and louder drawing near
The gnawing of their teeth he could hear.

And in at the windows and in at the door,
And through the walls helter-skelter they pour,
And down from the ceiling and up through the floor,
From the right and the left, from behind and before,
From within and without, from above and below,
And all at once to the Bishop they go.

They have whetted their teeth against the stones,
And now they pick the Bishop's bones;
They gnaw'd the flesh from every limb,
For they were sent to do judgement on him.

Westbury, 1799.

To a Bee

I

Thou wert out betimes, thou busy, busy Bee!
As abroad I took my early way,
Before the Cow from her resting-place
Had risen up and left her trace
On the meadow, with dew so gray,
Saw I thee, thou busy, busy Bee.

64

2
Thou wert working late, thou busy, busy Bee!
After the fall of the Cistus flower,
When the Primrose-of-evening was ready to burst,
I heard thee last, as I saw thee first;
In the silence of the evening hour,
Heard I thee, thou busy, busy Bee.

3
Thou art a miser, thou busy, busy Bee!
Late and early at employ;
Still on thy golden stores intent,
Thy summer in heaping and hoarding is spent
What thy winter will never enjoy;
Wise lesson this for me, thou busy, busy Bee!

4
Little dost thou think, thou busy, busy Bee!
What is the end of thy toil,
When the lastest flowers of the ivy are gone,
And all thy work for the year is done,
Thy master comes for the spoil.
Woe then for thee, thou busy, busy Bee!

Westbury, 1799.

The Amatory Poems of Abel Shufflebottom[1]

SONNET I

Delia at Play

She held a *Cup and Ball* of ivory white,
Less white the ivory than her *snowy* hand!
Enrapt, I watch'd her from my secret stand,
As now, intent, in *innocent* delight,
Her *taper* fingers twirl'd the giddy ball,
Now tost it, following still with EAGLE *sight*,
Now on the pointed end *infix'd* its fall.
Marking her sport I mused, and musing sigh'd,
Methought the BALL she play'd with was my HEART;
(Alas! that sport like *that* should be her pride!)
And the *keen point* which stedfast still she eyed
Wherewith to pierce it, that was CUPID'S *dart;*
Shall I not then the cruel Fair condemn
Who *on that dart* IMPALES *my* BOSOM'S GEM?

SONNET II

To a Painter attempting Delia's Portrait

Rash Painter! canst thou give the ORB OF DAY
In all its noontide glory? or portray
The DIAMOND, that athwart the *taper'd* hall
Flings the rich flashes of its dazzling light
Even if thine art could boast such *magic might,*

Yet if it strove to paint *my Angel's* EYE,
Here it perforce must fail. Cease! lest I call
Heaven's vengeance on thy sin: Must thou be told
The CRIME *it is to paint* DIVINITY?
Rash Painter! should the world her charms behold,
Dim and defiled, as there they needs must be,
They to their *old idolatry* would fall,
And bend before her form the *pagan* knee,
Fairer than VENUS, DAUGHTER OF THE SEA.

SONNET III

He proves the Existence of a Soul from his Love for Delia

SOME have denied a soul! THEY NEVER LOVED.
Far from my Delia now by fate removed,
At home, abroad, I view her everywhere;
Her ONLY in the FLOOD OF NOON I see,
My *Goddess-Maid*, my OMNIPRESENT FAIR,
For LOVE *annihilates the world to me!*
And when the weary SOL *around his bed*
Closes the SABLE CURTAINS *of the night*,
SUN OF MY SLUMBERS, on my dazzled sight
SHE shines confest. When *every sound is dead*,
The SPIRIT OF HER VOICE comes then *to roll*
The *surge of music* o'er my wavy brain.
Far, far from her my *Body* drags its chain,
But sure with Delia *I exist* A SOUL!

SONNET IV

The Poet expresses his Feelings respecting a Portrait in Delia's Parlour

I WOULD I were that portly Gentleman
With gold-laced hat and golden-headed cane,
Who hangs in Delia's parlour! For whene'er
From book or needlework her looks arise,
On him *converge the* SUN-BEAMS *of her eyes,*
And he *unblamed* may gaze upon MY FAIR,
And oft MY FAIR his *favoured* form surveys.
O HAPPY PICTURE! still on HER to gaze;
I envy him! and jealous fear alarms,
Lest the STRONG *glance* of those *divinest* charms
Warm HIM TO LIFE, as in the ancient days,
When MARBLE MELTED in Pygmalion's arms.
I would I were that portly Gentleman
With gold-laced hat and golden-headed cane.

Love Elegies.

Elegy I

THE POET RELATES HOW HE OBTAINED DELIA'S POCKET-HANDKERCHIEF

'T is mine! what accents can my joy declare?
  Blest be the pressure of the thronging rout!
Blest be the hand so hasty of my fair,
  That left the *tempting corner* hanging out!

I envy not the joy the pilgrim feels,
  After long travel to some distant shrine,
When at the relic of his saint he kneels,
  For Delia's POCKET-HANDKERCHIEF IS MINE.

When first with *filching fingers* I drew near,
  Keen hope shot tremulous through every vein,
And when the *finish'd deed* removed my fear,
  Scarce could my bounding heart its joy contain.

What though the Eighth Commandment rose to mind,
  It only served a moment's qualm to move;
For thefts like this it could not be design'd,
  The Eighth Commandment WAS NOT MADE FOR LOVE!

Here when she took the macaroons from me,
  She wiped her mouth to clean the crumbs so sweet!
Dear napkin! yes, she wiped her lips in thee!
  Lips *sweeter* than the *macaroons* she eat.

And when she took that pinch of Mocabaw,
  That made my Love *so delicately* sneeze,
Thee to her Roman nose applied I saw,
  And thou art doubly dear for things like these.

No washerwoman's filthy hand shall e'er,
  SWEET POCKET-HANDKERCHIEF! thy worth profane;
For thou hast touch'd the *rubies* of my fair,
  And I will kiss thee o'er and o'er again.

Elegy II

THE POET INVOKES THE SPIRITS OF THE ELEMENTS
TO APPROACH DELIA.—HE DESCRIBES HER SINGING

Ye SYLPHS, who *banquet* on my Delia's blush,
  Who on her locks of FLOATING GOLD repose.
Dip in her cheek your GOSSAMERY BRUSH,
  And with its bloom of beauty *tinge* THE ROSE.

Hover around her lips on *rainbow wing*,
  Load from her honey'd breath your *viewless* feet,
Bear thence a richer fragrance for the Spring,
  And make the lily and the violet sweet.

Ye GNOMES, whose toil through many a dateless year
  Its nurture to the infant gem supplies,
From central caverns bring your diamonds here,
  To *ripen in the* SUN OF DELIA'S EYES.

And ye who bathe in Etna's lava springs,
  Spirits of fire! to see my love advance;
Fly, SALAMANDERS, on ASBESTOS' wings,
  To wanton in my Delia's *fiery* glance.

She weeps, she weeps! her eye with anguish swells,
  Some tale of sorrow melts my FEELING GIRL!
NYMPHS! catch the tears, and in your lucid shells
  Enclose them, EMBRYOS OF THE ORIENT PEARL.

She sings! the Nightingale with envy hears,
  The CHERUB listens from his starry throne,
And motionless are stopt the attentive SPHERES,
  To hear *more heavenly music* than their own.

Cease, Delia, cease! for all the ANGEL THRONG,
  Hearkening to thee, let sleep their golden wires!
Cease, Delia, cease that *too surpassing* song,
  Lest, *stung to envy*, they should break their lyres.

Cease, ere my senses are to madness driven
  By the strong joy! Cease, Delia, lest my soul,
Enrapt, already THINK ITSELF IN HEAVEN,
  And burst the feeble Body's frail controul.

Elegy III

The comb between whose ivory teeth she strains
 The straightening curls of gold so *beamy bright*,
Not spotless merely from the touch remains,
 But issues forth *more pure*, more *milky white*.

The rose-pomatum that the FRISEUR spreads
 Sometimes with honour'd fingers for my fair
No added perfume on her tresses sheds,
 But borrows sweetness from her sweeter hair.

Happy the FRISEUR who in Delia's hair
 With licensed fingers uncontroul'd may rove!
And happy in his death the DANCING BEAR,
 Who died to make pomatum for my LOVE.

Oh could I hope that e'er my favour'd lays
 Might *curl those lovely locks* with conscious pride,
Nor Hammond,* nor the Mantuan Shepherd's praise,
 I'd envy then, nor wish reward beside.

Cupid has strung from you, O tresses fine,
 The bow that in my breast impell'd his dart;
From you, sweet locks! he wove the subtile line
 Wherewith the urchin *angled for* MY HEART.

Fine are my Delia's tresses as the threads
 That from the silk-worm, *self-interr'd*, proceed;
Fine as the GLEAMY GOSSAMER that spreads
 Its filmy web-work o'er the tangled mead.

[*James Hammond, whose *Love Elegies*, 1743, Johnson in his *Lives* of
the poets described as lacking passion, nature and manners, with 'few
sentiments drawn from nature, and few images from modern life.']

Yet with these tresses Cupid's power elate
  My captive *heart* has *handcuff'd* in a chain,
Strong as the cables of some huge first-rate,
  THAT BEARS BRITANNIA'S THUNDERS O'ER THE MAIN.

The SYLPHS that round her radiant locks repair,
  In *flowing lustre* bathe their brightening wings;
And ELFIN MINSTRELS with assiduous care
  The ringlets rob for FAERY FIDDLE-STRINGS.

Elegy IV

THE POET RELATES HOW HE STOLE A LOCK OF
DELIA'S HAIR, AND HER ANGER

Oh! be the day accurst that gave me birth!
  Ye Seas, to swallow me in kindness rise!
Fall on me, Mountains! and thou merciful Earth,
  Open, and hide me from my Delia's eyes!

Let universal Chaos now return,
  Now let the central fires their prison burst,
And EARTH and HEAVEN and AIR and OCEAN burn . . .
  For Delia FROWNS . . SHE FROWNS, *and I am curst!*

Oh! I could dare the fury of the fight,
  Where hostile MILLIONS sought my single life;
Would storm VOLCANO BATTERIES with delight,
  And grapple with GRIM DEATH in glorious strife.

Oh! I could brave the bolts of angry JOVE,
  When ceaseless lightnings fire the midnight skies;
What is *his wrath* to that of HER I love?
  What is his LIGHTNING to my DELIA'S EYES?

Go, fatal lock! I cast thee to the wind;
  Ye *serpent* CURLS, ye *poison-tendrils*, go!
Would I could tear they memory from my mind,
  ACCURSED LOCK, . . thou cause of all my woe!

Seize the CURST CURLS, ye Furies, as they fly!
  Demons of Darkness, guard the infernal roll,
That thence your cruel vengeance when I die,
  May *knit the* KNOTS OF TORTURE *for my* SOUL.

Last night, . . Oh hear me, Heaven, and grant my prayer!
  The BOOK OF FATE before thy suppliant lay,
And let me from its ample records tear
  Only the single PAGE OF YESTERDAY!

Or let me meet OLD TIME upon his flight,
  And I will STOP HIM on his restless way;
Omnipotent in Love's resistless might,
  I'll force him back the ROAD OF YESTERDAY.

Last night, as o'er the page of Love's despair,
  My Delia bent *deliciously* to grieve,
I stood a *treacherous loiterer* by her chair,
  And drew the FATAL SCISSORS from my sleeve:

And would that at that instant o'er my thread
  The SHEARS OF ATROPOS had open'd then;
And when I reft the lock from Delia's head,
  Had cut me sudden from the sons of men!

She heard the scissors that fair lock divide,
  And whilst my heart with transport panted big,
She cast a FURY frown on me, and cried,
  'You stupid Puppy, . . you have spoil'd my Wig!'

Westbury, 1799.

73

The Old Man's Comforts

AND HOW HE GAINED THEM

You are old, Father William the young man cried,
The few locks which are left you are grey;
You are hale, Father William, a hearty old man,
Now tell me the reason, I pray.

In the days of my youth, Father William replied,
I remember'd that youth would fly fast,
And abused not my health and my vigour at first,
That I never might need them at last.

You are old, Father William, the young man cried,
And pleasures with youth pass away;
And yet you lament not the days that are gone,
Now tell me the reason, I pray.

In the days of my youth, Father William replied,
I remember'd that youth could not last;
I thought of the future, whatever I did,
That I never might grieve for the past.

You are old, Father William, the young man cried,
And life must be hastening away;
You are cheerful, and love to converse upon death,
Now tell me the reason, I pray.

I am cheerful, young man, Father William replied,
Let the cause thy attention engage;
In the days of my youth I remember'd my God!
And He hath not forgotten my age.

Westbury, 1799.

The Pig

A COLLOQUIAL POEM

Jacob! I do not like to see thy nose
Turn'd up in scornful curve at yonder Pig.
It would be well, my friend, if we, like him,
Were perfect in our kind! . . And why despise
The sow-born grunter? . . He is obstinate,
Thou answerest; ugly, and the filthiest beast
That banquets upon offal. . . . . Now I pray you
Hear the Pig's Counsel.
                     Is he obstinate?
We must not, Jacob, be deceived by words;
We must not take them as unheeding hands
Receive base money at the current worth,
But with a just suspicion try their sound,
And in the even balance weigh them well.
See now to what this obstinacy comes:
A poor, mistreated, democratic beast,
He knows that his unmerciful drivers seek
Their profit, and not his. He hath not learnt
That Pigs were made for Man, . . born to be brawn'd
And baconized: that he must please to give
Just what his gracious masters please to take;
Perhaps his tusks, the weapons Nature gave
For self-defence, the general privilege;
Perhaps, . . hark Jacob! dost thou hear that horn?
Woe to the young posterity of Pork!
Their enemy is at hand.
                        Again. Thou say'st
The Pig is ugly. Jacob, look at him!
Those eyes have taught the Lover flattery.
His face, . . nay Jacob, Jacob! were it fair
To judge a Lady in her dishabille?
Fancy it drest, and with saltpetre rouged.
Behold his tail, my friend; with curls like that

The wanton hop marries her stately spouse:
So crisp in beauty Amoretta's hair
Rings round her lover's soul the chains of love.
And what is beauty, but the aptitude
Of parts harmonious? Give thy fancy scope,
And thou wilt find that no imagined change
Can beautify this beast. Place at his end
The starry glories of the Peacock's pride,
Give him the Swan's white breast; for his horn-hoofs
Shape such a foot and ankle as the waves
Crowded in eager rivalry to kiss
When Venus from the enamour'd sea arose; . .
Jacob, thou canst but make a monster of him!
All alteration man could think, would mar
His Pig-perfection.
               The last charge, . . he lives
A dirty life. Here I could shelter him
With noble and right-reverend precedents,
And show by sanction of authority
That 't is a very honourable thing
To thrive by dirty ways. But let me rest
On better ground the unanswerable defence.
The Pig is a philosopher, who knows
No prejudice. Dirt? . . Jacob, what is dirt?
If matter, . . why the delicate dish that tempts
An o'ergorged Epicure to the last morsel
That stuffs him to the throat-gates, is no more.
If matter be not, but as Sages say,
Spirit is all, and all things visible
Are one, the infinitely modified,
Think, Jacob, what that Pig is, and the mire
Wherein he stands knee-deep!
               And there! the breeze
Pleads with me, and has won thee to a smile
That speaks conviction. O'er yon blossom'd field
Of beans it came, and thoughts of bacon rise.

Westbury, 1799.

The Ebb Tide

Slowly thy flowing tide
Came in, old Avon! scarcely did mine eyes,
As watchfully I roam'd thy green-wood side,
    Perceive its gentle rise.

With many a stroke and strong
The labouring boatmen upward plied their oars,
Yet little way they made, though labouring long
    Between they winding shores.

Now down thine ebbing tide
The unlabour'd boat falls rapidly along;
The solitary helm's-man sits to guide,
    And sings an idle song.

Now o'er the rocks that lay
So silent late, the shallow current roars;
Fast flow thy waters on their seaward way
    Through wider-spreading shores.

Avon! I gaze and know
The lesson emblem'd in thy varying way;
It speaks of human joys that rise so slow,
    So rapidly decay.

Kingdoms which long have stood,
And slow to strength and power attain'd at last,
Thus from the summit of high fortune's flood
    They ebb to ruin fast.

Thus like thy flow appears
Time's tardy course to manhood's envied stage;
Alas! how hurryingly the ebbing years
    Then hasten to old age!

Westbury, 1799.

(Sonnet: Farewell to Martin Hall)

Farewell my home, my home no longer now.
Witness of many a calm and happy day;
And thou fair eminence, upon whose brow
Dwells the last sunshine of the evening ray,
Farewell! These eyes no longer shall pursue
The western sun beyond the farthest height,
When slowly he forsakes the fields of light.
No more the freshness of the falling dew,
Cool and delightful, here shall bathe my head,
As from this western window dear, I lean,
Listening, the while I watch the placid scene,
The martins twittering underneath the shed.
Farewell, dear home! where many a day has past
In joys whose loved remembrance long shall last.

Westbury, 1799.

(Sonnet: To Porlock)

Porlock, thy verdant vale so fair to sight,
Thy lofty hills which fern and furze embrown,
The waters that roll musically down
Thy woody glens, the traveller with delight
Recalls to memory, and the channel grey
Circling its surges in thy level bay.
Porlock, I also shall forget thee not,
Here by the unwelcome summer rain confined;
But often shall hereafter call to mind
How here, a patient prisoner, 't was my lot
To wear the lonely, lingering close of day,
Making my Sonnet by the alehouse fire,
Whilst Idleness and Solitude inspire
Dull rhymes to pass the duller hours away.

August, 1799.

The Devil's Thoughts

[This *jeu d'esprit* was made up jointly by Southey and Coleridge. Different versions were printed in their collected poems, Southey greatly expanding, though hardly improving, the original verson—as given here and as first printed in the *Morning Post* of September 6th., 1799—and changing the title to 'The Devil's Walk.' Southey in his extended version says that he and Coleridge wrote the poem at Nether Stowey—this would have been in August 1799—where Southey, it appears, began it with the opening stanzas while he was shaving; Coleridge joined in at breakfast.]

I

From his brimstone bed at break of day,
  A walking the Devil is gone,
To look at his snug little farm the Earth,
  And see how his stock went on.

II

Over the hill and over the dale,
  And he went over the plain,
And backward and forward he swish'd his long tail,
  As a Gentleman swishes his cane.

III

He saw a Lawyer killing a viper
  On a dunghill beside his stable;
'Oh—oh,' quoth he, for it put him in mind
  Of the story of Cain and Abel.

IV

An apothecary on a white horse
   Rode by on his vocation;
And the Devil thought of his old friend
   Death, in the Revelation.[1]

V

He went into a rich bookseller's shop,
   Quoth he, 'We are both of one college!
For I sate myself, like a cormorant, once
   Hard by the tree of Knowledge.'[2]

VI

He saw a Turnkey in a trice
   Hand-cuff a troublesome blade—
'Nimbly,' quoth he, 'do the fingers move
   If a man be but us'd to his trade.'

VII

He saw the same turnkey unfettering a man
   With but little expedition,
And he laugh'd, for he thought of the long debates
   On the Slave Trade Abolition.

[1] 'And I looked, and behold a pale horse: and his name that sat on him was Death.'—Rev. ch. vi. 8.

[2] This anecdote is related by that most interesting of the Devil's Biographers, Mr. John Milton, in his *Paradise Lost*, and we have here the Devil's own testimony to the truth and accuracy of it.

VIII

As he went through —— ——[1] fields he look'd
    At a solitary cell—
And the Devil was pleas'd, for it gave him a hint
    For improving the prisons of Hell.

IX

He past a cottage with a double coach-house,
    A cottage of gentility,
And he grinn'd at the sight, for his favourite vice
    Is pride that apes humility.

X

He saw a pig right rapidly
    Adown the river float,
The pig swam well, but every stroke
    Was cutting his own throat.

XI

Old Nicholas grinn'd, and swish'd his tail
    For joy and admiration—
And he thought of his daughter, Victory,
    And her darling babe, Taxation.

XII

He met an old acquaintance
    Just by the Methodist meeting;
She held a consecrated flag,
    And the Devil nods a greeting.

[[1] In the later versions by Coleridge and Southey these blanks are filled in as 'Cold-Bath', i.e. Cold-Bath Fields Prison in Clerkenwell, London. There was much talk at this time of the general introduction of confinement in cells, following Howard's suggestions for prison reform. It had been made possible by the Prisons Act, 1791.]

XIII

She tip'd him the wink, then frown'd and cri'd,
  'Avaunt! my name's ——.'¹
And turn'd to Mr. ——
  And leer'd like a love-sick pigeon.

XIV

General ——'s burning face
  He saw with consternation,
And back to Hell his way did take,
For the Devil thought by a slight mistake,
  It was General Conflagration.

Gooseberry-Pie

A PINDARIC ODE

I

Gooseberry-Pie is best.
Full of the theme, O Muse, begin the song!
  What though the sunbeams of the West
  Mature within the Turtle's breast
Blood glutinous and fat of verdant hue?
What though the Deer bound sportively along
O'er springey turf, the Park's elastic vest?
  Give them their honours due, . .
  But Gooseberry-Pie is best.

[¹ Southey in his later version fills the blank as 'Religion'.]

82

2

Behind his oxen slow
The patient Ploughman plods,
And as the Sower followed by the clods
Earth's genial womb received the living seed.
The rains descend, the grains they grow;
Saw ye the vegetable ocean
Roll its green ripple to the April gale?
The golden waves with multitudinous motion
Swell o'er the summer vale?

3

It flows through Alder banks along
Beneath the copse that hides the hill;
The gentle stream you cannot see,
You only hear its melody,
The stream that turns the Mill.
Pass on a little way, pass on,
And you shall catch its gleam anon;
And hark! the loud and agonizing groan
That makes its anguish known,
Where tortured by the Tyrant Lord of Meal
The Brook is broken on the Wheel!

4

Blow fair, blow fair, thou orient gale!
On the white bosom of the sail
Ye Winds enamour'd lingering lie!
Ye Waves of ocean spare the bark,
Ye Tempests of the sky!
From distant realms she comes to bring
The sugar for my Pie.
For this on Gambia's arid side
The Vulture's feet are scaled with blood,
And Beelzebub beholds with pride,
His darling planter brood.

First in the spring thy leaves were seen,
Thou beauteous bush, so early green!
Soon ceased thy blossoms' little life of love.
O safer than the gold-fruit-bearing tree
The glory of that old Hesperian grove, . .
No Dragon does there need for thee
With quintessential sting to work alarms,
Prepotent guardian of thy fruitage fine,
Thou vegetable Porcupine! . . .
And didst thou scratch thy tender arms,
O Jane! that I should dine!

6
The flour, the sugar, and the fruit,
Commingled well, how well they suit,
And they were well bestow'd.
O Jane, with truth I praise your Pie
And will not you in just reply
Praise my Pindaric Ode?

Exeter, 1799.

The King of the Crocodiles

The people at Isna, in Upper Egypt, have a superstition con-
cerning Crocodiles similar to that entertained in the West
Indies; they say there is a King of them who resides near
Isna, and who has ears, but no tail; and he possesses an
uncommon regal quality, that of doing no harm. Some
are bold enough to assert that they have seen him. Brown's
Travels.

If the Crocodile Dynasty in Egypt had been described as
distinguished by a long neck, as well as the want of a tail,
it might be supposed that some tradition of the Ichthyo-
saurus, or other variety of the Praeadamite Crocodile, was
preserved in those countries.

No one who has perused Mr. Waterton's *Wanderings* will
think there is any thing more extraordinary in the woman's
attack upon her intended devourer, than in what that enter-
prising and most observant naturalist has himself performed.
He has ridden a Crocodile, twisting the huge reptile's fore-
legs on his back by main force, and using them as a bridle.
'Should it be asked', he says, 'how I managed to keep my
seat, I would answer, I hunted some years with Lord
Darlington's fox-hounds.'
There is a translation of this ballad by Bilderdijk, published
his *Krekelzangen*, 1822, vol. ii. p. 109, before the second part
was written.

PART I

'Now, Woman, why without your veil?
And wherefore do you look so pale?
And, Woman, why do you groan so sadly,
And wherefore beat your bosom madly?'

'Oh! I have lost my darling boy,
In whom my soul had all its joy;
And I for sorrow have torn my veil,
And sorrow hath made my very heart pale.

'Oh, I have lost my darling child,
And that's the loss that makes me wild;
He stoop'd to the river down to drink,
And there was a Crocodile by the brink.

'He did not venture in to swim,
He only stoopt to drink at the brim;
But under the reeds the Crocodile lay,
And struck with his tail and swept him away.

85

'Now take me in your boat, I pray,
For down the river lies my way,
And me to the Reed-Island bring,
For I will go to the Crocodile King.

'He reigns not now in Crocodilople,
Proud as the Turk at Constantinople;
No ruins of his great City remain,
The Island of Reeds is his whole domain.

'Like a Dervise there he passes his days,
Turns up his eyes, and fasts and prays;
And being grown pious and meek and mild,
He now never eats man, woman, or child.

'The King of the Crocodiles never does wrong,
He has no tail so stiff and strong,
He has no tail to strike and slay,
But he has ears to hear what I say.

'And to the King I will complain,
How my poor child was wickedly slain;
The King of the Crocodiles he is good,
And I shall have the murderer's blood.'

The man replied, 'No, Woman, no,
To the Island of Reeds I will not go;
I would not for any worldly thing
See the face of the Crocodile King.'

'Then lend me now your little boat,
And I will down the river float.
I tell thee that no worldly thing
Shall keep me from the Crocodile King.

'The King of the Crocodiles he is good,
And therefore will give me blood for blood;
Being so mighty and so just,
He can revenge me, he will, and he must.'

The Woman she leapt into the boat,
And down the river alone she did float,
And fast with the stream the boat proceeds,
And now she is come to the Island of Reeds.

The King of the Crocodiles there was seen,
He sat upon the eggs of the Queen,
And all around, a numerous rout,
The young Prince Crocodiles crawl'd about.

The Woman shook every limb with fear,
As she to the Crocodile King came near,
For never man without fear and awe
The face of his Crocodile Majesty saw.

She fell upon her bended knee,
And said, 'O King, have pity on me,
For I have lost my darling child,
And that's the loss that makes me wild.

'A Crocodile ate him for his food;
Now let me have the murderer's blood;
Let me have vengeance for my boy,
The only thing that can give me joy.

'I know that you, Sire! never do wrong,
You have no tail so stiff and strong,
You have no tail to strike and slay,
But you have ears to hear what I say.'

'You have done well,' the King replies,
And fix'd on her his little eyes;
'Good Woman, yes, you have done right,
But you have not described me quite.

'I have no tail to strike and slay,
And I have ears to hear what you say;
I have teeth, moreover, as you may see,
And I will make a meal of thee.'

Bristol, 1799.
87

PART II

Wicked the word and bootless the boast,
As cruel King Crocodile found to his cost,
And proper reward of tyrannical might,
He show'd his teeth, but he miss'd his bite.

'A meal of me!' the Woman cried,
Taking wit in her anger, and courage beside;
She took him his forelegs and hind between,
And trundled him off the eggs of the Queen.

To revenge herself then she did not fail,
He was slow in his motions for want of a tail;
But well for the Woman was it, the while,
That the Queen was gadding abroad in the Nile.

Two crocodile Princes, as they play'd on the sand,
She caught, and grasping them one in each hand,
Thrust the head of one into the throat of the other,
And made each Prince Crocodile choke his brother.

And when she had truss'd three couple this way,
She carried them off, and hasten'd away,
And plying her oars with might and main,
Cross'd the river and got to the shore again.

When the Crocodile Queen came home, she found
That her eggs were broken and scattered around,
And that six young Princes, darlings all,
Were missing, for none of them answer'd her call.

Then many a not very pleasant thing
Pass'd between her and the Crocodile King:
'Is this your care of the nest,' cried she;
'It comes of your gadding abroad,' said he.

The Queen had the better in this dispute,
And the Crocodile King found it best to be mute,
While a terrible peal in his ears she rung,
For the Queen had a tail as well as a tongue.

In woeful patience he let her rail,
Standing less in fear of her tongue than her tail,
And knowing that all the words which were spoken
Could not mend one of the eggs that were broken.

The Woman, meantime, was very well pleased
She saved her life, and her heart was eased:
The justice she ask'd in vain for her son,
She had taken herself, and six for one.

'Mash-Allah!' her neighbours exclaim'd in delight:
She gave them a funeral supper that night,
Where they all agreed that revenge was sweet,
And young Prince Crocodiles delicate meat.

The Inchcape Rock

An older writer mentions a curious tradition which may be
worth quoting. 'By east the Isle of May', says he, 'twelve
miles from all land in the German seas, lyes a great hidden
rock, called Inchcape, very dangerous for navigators,
because it is overflowed everie tide. It is reported in old
times, upon the saide rock there was a bell, fixed upon a
tree or timber, which rang continually, being moved by the
sea, giving notice to the saylers of the danger. This bell or
clocke was put there and maintained by the Abbot of
Aberbrothok, and being taken down by a sea pirate, a yeare
thereafter he perished upon the same rocke, with ship and
goodes, in the righteous judgement of God.'—STODDART'S
Remarks on Scotland.

No stir in the air, no stir in the sea,
The ship was still as she could be,
Her sails from heaven received no motion,
Her keel was steady in the ocean.

Without either sign or sound of their shock
The waves flow'd over the Inchcape Rock;
So little they rose, so little they fell,
They did not move the Inchcape Bell.

The Abbot of Aberbrothok
Had placed that bell on the Inchcape Rock;
On a buoy in the storm it floated and swung,
And over the waves its warning rung.

When the Rock was hid by the surge's swell,
The mariners heard the warning bell;
And then they knew the perilous Rock,
And blest the Abbot of Aberbrothok.

The Sun in heaven was shining gay,
All things were joyful on that day;
The sea-birds scream'd as they wheel'd round,
And there was joyaunce in their sound.

The buoy of the Inchcape Bell was seen
A darker speck on the ocean green;
Sir Ralph the Rover walk'd his deck,
And he fix'd his eye on the darker speck.

He felt the cheering power of spring,
It made him whistle, it made him sing;
His heart was mirthful to excess,
But the Rover's mirth was wickedness.

His eye was on the Inchcape float;
Quoth he, 'My men, put out the boat,
And row me to the Inchcape Rock,
And I'll plague the Abbot of Aberbrothok.'

The boat is lower'd, the boatmen row,
And to the Inchcape Rock they go;
Sir Ralph bent over from the boat,
And he cut the Bell from the Inchcape float.

Down sunk the Bell with a gurgling sound,
The bubbles rose and burst around;
Quoth Sir Ralph, 'The next who comes to the Rock
Won't bless the Abbot of Aberbrothok.'

Sir Ralph the Rover sail'd away,
He scour'd the seas for many a day;
And now grown rich with plunder'd store,
He steers his course for Scotland's shore.

So thick a haze o'erspreads the sky
They cannot see the Sun on high;
The wind hath blown a gale all day,
At evening it hath died away.

On the deck the Rover takes his stand,
So dark it is they see no land.
Quoth Sir Ralph, 'It will be lighter soon,
For there is the dawn of the rising Moon.'

'Canst hear,' said one, 'the breakers roar?
For methinks we should be near the shore.'
'Now where we are I cannot tell,
But I wish I could hear the Inchcape Bell.'

They hear no sound, the swell is strong;
Though the wind hath fallen they drift along,
Till the vessel strikes with a shivering shock,—
'Oh Christ! it is the Inchcape Rock!'

Sir Ralph the Rover tore his hair;
He curst himself in his despair;
The waves rush in on every side,
The ship is sinking beneath the tide.

But even in his dying fear
One dreadful sound could the Rover hear,
A sound as if with the Inchcape Bell,
The Devil below was ringing his knell.

Bristol, 1802.

The Alderman's Funeral

STRANGER

Whom are they ushering from the world, with all
This pageantry and long parade of death?

TOWNSMAN

A long parade, indeed, Sir, and yet here
You see but half; round yonder bend it reaches
A furlong further, carriage behind carriage.

STRANGER

'T is but a mournful sight, and yet the pomp
Tempts me to stand a gazer.

TOWNSMAN

                                Yonder schoolboy
Who plays the truant, says the proclamation
Of peace was nothing to the show; and even
The chairing of the members at election
Would not have been a finer sight than this;
Only that red and green are prettier colours
Than all this mourning. There, Sir, you behold
One of the red-gown'd worthies of the city,
The envy and the boast of our exchange; . . .
Aye, what was worth, last week, a good half-million,
Screw'd down in yonder hearse!

STRANGER
                              Then he was born
Under a lucky planet, who to-day
Puts mourning on for his inheritance.

TOWNSMAN
When first I heard his death, that very wish
Leapt to my lips; but now the closing scene
Of the comedy hath waken'd wiser thoughts;
And I bless God, that, when I go to the grave,
There will not be the weight of wealth like his
To sink me down.

STRANGER
                    The camel and the needle, . .
Is that then in your mind?

TOWNSMAN
                              Even so. The text
Is Gospel-Wisdom. I would ride the camel, . .
Yea leap him flying, through the needle's eye,
As easily as such a pamper'd soul
Could pass the narrow gate.

STRANGER
                         Your pardon, Sir,
But sure this lack of Christian charity
Looks not like Christian truth.

TOWNSMAN
                              Your pardon too, Sir,
If, with this text before me, I should feel
In the preaching mood! But for these barren fig-trees,
With all their flourish and their leafiness,
We have been told their destiny and use,
When the axe is laid unto the root, and they
Cumber the earth no longer.

93

STRANGER

                              Was his wealth
Stored fraudfully, . . the spoil of orphans wrong'd,
And widows who had none to plead their right?

TOWNSMAN

All honest, open, honourable gains,
All legal interest, bonds and mortgages,
Ships to the East and West.

STRANGER

                              Why judge you then
So hardly of the dead?

TOWNSMAN

                              For what he left
Undone; . . for sins, not one of which is written
In the Ten Commandments. He, I warrant him,
Believed no other Gods than those of the Creed;
Bow'd to no idols, . . but his money-bags;
Swore no false oaths, except at the custom-house;
Kept the Sabbath idle; built a monument
To honour his dead father; did not murder;
Never sustain'd an action for crim-con;
Never pick'd pockets; never bore false-witness;
And never, with that all-commanding wealth,
Coveted his neighbour's house, nor ox, nor ass!

STRANGER

You knew him then it seems?

TOWNSMAN

                              As all men know
The virtues of your hundred-thousanders;
They never hide their lights beneath a bushel.

94

STRANGER

Nay, nay, uncharitable Sir! for often
Doth bounty like a streamlet flow unseen,
Freshening and giving life along its course.

TOWNSMAN

We track the streamlet by the brighter green
And livelier growth it gives; . . but as for this . .
This was a pool that stagnated and stunk;
The rains of heaven engendered nothing in it
But slime and foul corruption.

STRANGER
                                    Yet even these
Are reservoirs whence public charity
Still keeps her channels full.

TOWNSMAN
                                    Now, Sir, you touch
Upon the point. This man of half a million
Had all these public virtues which you praise;
But the poor man rung never at his door,
And the old beggar, at the public gate,
Who, all the summer long, stands hat in hand,
He knew how vain it was to lift an eye
To that hard face. Yet he was always found
Among your ten and twenty pound subscribers,
Your benefactors in the newspapers.
His alms were money put to interest
In the other world, . . donations to keep open
A running charity account with heaven, . .
Retaining fees against the Last Assizes,
When, for the trusted talents, strict account
Shall be required from all, and the old Arch-Lawyer
Plead his own cause as plaintiff.

STRANGER
                                    I must needs
Believe you, Sir: . . these are your witnesses,
These mourners here, who from their carriages
Gape at the gaping crowd. A good March wind
Were to be pray'd for now, to lend their eyes
Some decent rheum; the very hireling mute
Bears not a face more blank of all emotion
Than the old servant of the family!
How can this man have lived, that thus his death
Costs not the soiling one white handkerchief!

TOWNSMAN
Who should lament for him, Sir, in whose heart
Love had no place, nor natural charity?
The parlour spaniel, when she heard his step,
Rose slowly from the hearth, and stole aside
With creeping pace; she never raised her eyes
To woo kind words from him, not laid her head
Upraised upon his knee with fondling whime.
How could it be but thus? Arithmetic
Was the sole science he was ever taught;
The multiplication-table was his Creed,
His Pater-noster, and his Decalogue.
When yet he was a boy, and should have breathed
The open air and sunshine of the fields,
To give his blood its natural spring and play,
He in a close and dusky counting-house
Smoke-dried and sear'd and shrivell'd up his heart.
So from the way in which he was train'd up
His feet departed not; he toil'd and moil'd,
Poor muck-worm! through his three-score years and ten;
And when the earth shall now be shovell'd on him,
If that which served him for a soul were still
Within it's husk, 't would still be dirt to dirt.

STRANGER

Yet your next newspapers will blazon him
For industry and honourable wealth
A bright example.

TOWNSMAN

Even half a million
Gets him no other praise. But come this way
Some twelve months hence, and you will find his virtues
Trimly set forth in lapidary lines,
Faith with her torch beside, and little Cupids
Dropping upon his urn their marble tears.

Bristol, 1803.

(The Submarine Garden)

FROM 'THE CURSE OF KEHAMA'

It was a Garden still beyond all price,
Even yet it was a place of Paradise;
For where the mighty Ocean could not spare,
There had he with his own creation,
Sought to repair his work of devastation.
And here were coral bowers,
And grots of madrepores,
And banks of sponge, as soft and fair to eye
As e'er was mossy bed
Whereon the Wood Nymphs lie
With languid limbs in summer's sultry hours.
Here too were living flowers
Which, like a bud compacted,
Their purple cups contracted,
And now in open blossom spread,

G   97

Stretch'd like green anthers many a seeking head.
And arborets of jointed stone were there,
And plants of fibres fine, as silkworm's thread;
Yea, beautiful as Mermaid's golden hair
Upon the waves dispread.
Others that, like the broad banana growing,
Raised their long wrinkled leaves of purple hue,
Like streamers wide out-flowing
And whatsoe'er the depths of Ocean hide
From human eyes, Ladurlad[1] there espied,
Trees of the deep, and shrubs and fruits and flowers,
As fair as ours,
Wherewith the Sea-Nymphs love their locks to braid,
When to their father's hall, at festival
Repairing they, in emulous array,
Their charms display,
To grace the banquet, and the solemn day.

The golden fountains had not ceased to flow:
And where they mingled with the briny Sea,
There was a sight of wonder and delight,
To see the fish, like birds in air,
Above Ladurlad flying,
Round those strange waters they repair,
Their scarlet fins outspread and plying,
They float with gentle hovering there;
And now upon those little wings,
As if to dare forbidden things,
With wilful purpose bent,
Swift as an arrow from a bow,
They shoot across, and to and fro,
In rapid glance, like lightning go
Through that unwonted element.

[*Published* 1810]

[1 The moral hero of the epic, who labours under the curse of
Kehamà, the great Raja.]

The Poet's Pilgrimage:[1]

Proem

1

Once more I see thee, Skiddaw! once again
  Behold thee in thy majesty serene,
Where like the bulwark of this favour'd plain,
  Alone thou standest, monarch of the scene . . .
Thou glorious mountain, on whose ample breast
The sunbeams love to play, the vapours love to rest!

2

Once more, O Derwent, to thy aweful shores
  I come, insatiate of the accustom'd sight;
And listening as the eternal torrent roars,
  Drink in with eye and ear a fresh delight:
For I have wander'd far by land and sea,
In all my wanderings still remembering thee.

3

Twelve years (how large a part of man's brief day?)
  Nor idly, nor ingloriously spent,
Of evil and of good have held their way,
  Since first upon thy banks I pitch'd my tent.
Hither I came in manhood's active prime,
And here my head hath felt the touch of time.

4

Heaven hath with goodly increase blest me here,
  Where childless and opprest with grief I came;
With voice of fevent thankfulness sincere
  Let me the blessings which are mine proclaim:
Here I possess, . . what more should I require?
Books, children, leisure, . . all my heart's desire.

[1 See Introduction, page 19.]

5

O joyful hour, when to our longing home
  The long-expected wheels at length drew nigh!
When the first sound went forth, 'They come, they come!'
  And hope's impatience quicken'd every eye!
'Never had man whom Heaven would heap with bliss
More glad return, more happy hour than this.'

6

Aloft on yonder bench, with arms dispread,
  My boy stood, shouting there his father's name,
Waving his hat around his happy head;
  And there, a younger group, his sisters came:
Smiling they stood with looks of pleased surprize,
While tears of joy were seen in elder eyes.

7

Soon each and all came crouding round to share
  The cordial greeting, the beloved sight;
What welcomings of hand and lip were there!
  And when those overflowings of delight
Subsided to a sense of quiet bliss,
Life hath no purer deeper happiness.

8

The young companion of our weary way
  Found here the end desired of all her ills;
She who in sickness pining many a day
  Hunger'd and thirsted for her native hills,
Forgetful now of sufferings past and pain,
Rejoiced to see her own dear home again.

9

Recover'd now, the homesick mountaineer
  Sate by the playmate of her infancy,
Her twin-like comrade, . . render'd doubly dear
  For that long absence: full of life was she,
With voluble discourse and eager mien
Telling of all the wonders she had seen.

Here silently between her parents stood
  My dark-eyed Bertha, timid as a dove;
And gently oft from time to time she woo'd
  Pressure of hand, or word, or look of love,
With impulse shy of bashful tenderness,
Soliciting again the wish'd caress.

The younger twain in wonder lost were they,
  My gentle Kate, and my sweet Isabel:
Long of our promised coming, day by day
  It had been their delight to hear and tell;
And now when that long-promised hour was come,
Surprise and wakening memory held them dumb.

For in the infant mind, as in the old,
  When to its second childhood life declines,
A dim and troubled power doth Memory hold:
  But soon the light of young Remembrance shines
Renew'd, and influences of dormant love
Waken'd within, with quickening influence move.

O happy season theirs, when absence brings
  Small feeling of privation, none of pain,
Yet at the present object love re-springs,
  As night-closed flowers at morn expand again!
Nor deem our second infancy unblest,
When gradually composed we sink to rest.

Soon they grew blithe as they were wont to be;
  Her old endearments each began to seek:
And Isabel drew near to climb my knee,
  And pat with fondling hand her father's cheek
With voice and touch and look reviving thus
The feelings which had slept in long disuse.

But there stood one whose heart could entertain
  And comprehend the fullness of the joy;
The father, teacher, playmate, was again
  Come to his only and his studious boy:
And he beheld again that mother's eye,
Which with such ceaseless care had watch'd his infancy.

Bring forth the treasures now, . . a proud display, . .
  For rich as Eastern merchants we return!
Behold the black Beguine, the Sister grey,
  The Friars whose heads with sober motion turn,
The Ark well-fill'd all with its numerous hives,
Noah and Shem and Ham and Japhet, and their wives.

The tumbler, loose of limb; the wrestlers twain;
  And many a toy beside of quaint device,
Which, when his fleecy troops no more can gain
  Their pasture on the mountains hoar with ice,
The German shepherd carves with curious knife,
Earning in easy toil the food of frugal life.

It was a group which Richter, had he view'd,
  Might have deem'd worthy of his perfect skill;
The keen impatience of the younger brood,
  Their eager eyes and fingers never still;
The hope, the wonder, and the restless joy
Of those glad girls, and that vociferous boy!

The aged friend serene with quiet smile,
  Who in their pleasure finds her own delight;
The mother's heart-felt happiness the while;
  The aunts, rejoicing in the joyful sight;
And he who in his gaiety of heart,
With glib and noisy tongue perform'd the showman's part.

20

Scoff ye who will! but let me, gracious Heaven,
  Preserve this boyish heart till life's last day!
For so that inward light by Nature given
  Shall still direct, and cheer me on my way,
And brightening as the shades of age descend,
Shine forth with heavenly radiance at the end.

21

This was the morning light vouchsafed, which led
  My favour'd footsteps to the Muses' hill,
Whose arduous paths I have not ceased to tread,
  From good to better persevering still;
And if but self-approved, to praise or blame
Indifferent, while I toil for lasting fame.

22

And O ye nymphs of Castaly divine!
  Whom I have dutifully served so long,
Benignant to your votary now incline,
  That I may win your ear with gentle song,
Such as, I ween, is ne'er disown'd by you, . .
  A low prelusive strain, to nature true.

23

But when I reach at themes of loftier thought,
  And tell of things surpassing earthly sense,
(Which by yourselves, O Muses, I am taught,)
  Then aid me with your fuller influence,
And to the height of that great argument,
Support my spirit in her strong ascent!

24

So **may** I boldly round my temples bind
  The laurel which my master Spenser wore;
And free in spirit as the mountain wind
  That makes my symphony in this lone hour,
No perishable song of triumph raise,
But sing in worthy strains my Country's praise.

[*Published* 1816]

Stanzas

1

My days among the Dead are past;
  Around me I behold,
Where 'er these casual eyes are cast,
  The mighty minds of old;
My never failing friends are they,
With whom I converse day by day.

2

With them I take delight in weal,
  And seek relief in woe;
And while I understand and feel
  How much to them I owe,
My cheeks have often been bedew'd
With tears of thoughtful gratitude.

3

My thoughts are with the Dead, with them
  I live in long-past years,
Their virtues love, their faults condemn,
  Partake their hopes and fears,
And from their lessons seek and find
Instruction with an humble mind.

4

My hopes are with the Dead, anon
My place with them will be,
And I with them shall travel on
Through all Futurity;
Yet leaving here a name, I trust,
That will not perish in the dust.

Keswick, 1818.

The Cataract of Lodore

DESCRIBED IN RHYMES FOR THE NURSERY

'How does the Water,
Come down at Lodore?'
My little boy ask'd me
Thus, once on a time;
And moreover he task'd me
To tell him in rhyme.
Anon at the word,
There first came one daughter
And then came another,
To second and third
The request of their brother,
And to hear how the Water
Comes down at Lodore,
With its rush and its roar.
As many a time
They had seen it before.
So I told them in rhyme,
For of rhymes I had store;
And 't was in my vocation
For their recreation
That I should sing;
Because I was Laureate
To them and the King.

From its sources which well
In the Tarn on the fell;
From its fountains
In the mountains,
It's rills and it's gills;
Through moss and through brake,
It runs and it creeps
For awhile, till it sleeps
In its own little Lake.
And thence at departing,
Awakening and starting,
It runs through the reeds
And away it proceeds,
Through meadow and glade,
In sun and in shade,
And through the wood-shelter,
Among crags in its flurry,
Helter-skelter,
Hurry-scurry.
Here it comes sparkling,
And there it lies darkling;
Now smoking and frothing
It's tumult and wrath in,
Till in this rapid race
On which it is bent,
It reaches the place
Of its steep descent.

The Cataract strong
Then plunges along,
Striking and raging
As if a war waging
Its caverns and rocks among:
Rising and leaping,
Sinking and creeping,
Selling and sweeping,
Showering and springing,
Flying and flinging,

Writhing and ringing,
Eddying and whisking,
Spouting and frisking,
Turning and twisting,
Around and around
With endless rebound;
Smiting and fighting
A sight to delight in;
Confounding, astounding,
Dizzying and deafening the ear with its sound.

Collecting, projecting,
Receding and speeding,
And shocking and rocking,
And darting and parting,
And threading and spreading,
And whizzing and hissing,
And dripping and skipping,
And hitting and splitting,
And shining and twining,
And rattling and battling
And shaking and quaking,
And pouring and roaring,
And waving and raving,
And tossing and crossing,
And flowing and going,
And running and stunning,
And foaming and roaming,
And dinning and spinning,
And dropping and hopping,
And working and jerking,
And guggling and struggling,
And heaving and cleaving,
And moaning and groaning;

And glittering and frittering,
And gathering and feathering,
And whitening and brightening,

And quivering and shivering,
And hurrying and skurrying,
And thundering and floundering;

Dividing and gliding and sliding,
And falling and brawling and sprawling,
And driving and riving and striving,
And sprinkling and twinkling and wrinkling,
And sounding and bounding and rounding,
And bubbling and troubling and doubling,
And grumbling and rumbling and tumbling,
And clattering and battering and shattering;

Retreating and beating and meeting and sheeting,
Delaying and straying and playing and spraying,
Advancing and prancing and glancing and dancing,
Recoiling, turmoiling and toiling and boiling,
And gleaming and streaming and steaming and beaming,
And rushing and flushing and brushing and gushing,
And flapping and rapping and clapping and slapping,
And curling and whirling and purling and twirling,
And thumping and plumping and bumping and jumping,
And dashing and flashing and splashing and clashing;
And so never ending, but always descending,
Sounds and motions for ever and ever are blending,
All at once and all o'er, with a mighty uproar,
And this way the Water comes down at Lodore.

Keswick, 1890.

From A Vision of Judgement

'Twas at that sober hour when the light of day is receding,
And from surrounding things the hues wherewith day has
    adorn'd them
Fade, like the hopes of youth, till the beauty of earth is departed:

Pensive, though not in thought, I stood at the window beholding
Mountain and lake and vale; the valley disrobed of its verdure;
Derwent retaining yet from eve a glassy reflection
Where his expanded breast, then still and smooth as a mirror,
Under the woods reposed; the hills that, calm and majestic,
Lifted their heads in the silent sky, from far Glaramara
Bleacrag and Maidenmawr, to Grizedal and westermost Withop.
Dark and distinct they rose. The clouds had gather'd above them
High in the middle air, huge, purple, pillowy masses,
While in the west beyond was the last pale tint of the twilight;
Green as a stream in the glen whose pure and chrysolite waters
Flow o'er a schistous bed, and serene as the age of the righteous.
Earth was hush'd and still; all motion and sound were suspended:
Neither man was heard, bird, beast, nor humming of insect,
Only the voice of the Greta, heard only when all is in stillness.
Pensive I stood and alone, the hour and the scene had subdued me,
And as I gazed in the west, where Infinity seem'd to be open,
Yearn'd to be free from time, and felt that this life is a thraldom.

[*Published* 1821]

Robert the Rhymer's
True and Particular Account of Himself

Robert the Rhymer who lives at the Lakes
Describes himself thus, to prevent mistakes;
Or rather, perhaps, be it said, to correct them,
There, being plenty about for those who collect them.
He is lean of body, and lank of limb;
The man must walk fast who would overtake him.
His eyes are not yet much the worse for the wear,

And Time has not thinn'd nor straighten'd his hair,
Notwithstanding that now he is more than halfway
On the road from Grizzle to Gray.
He hath a long nose with a bending ridge;
It might be worthy of notice on Strasburg bridge.
He sings like a lark when at morn he arises,
And when evening comes he nightingalizes,
Warbling house-notes wild from throat and gizzard,
Which reach from A to G, and from G to Izzard.
His voice is as good as when he was young,
And he has teeth enough left to keep-in his tongue.
A man he is by nature merry,
Somewhat Tom-foolish, and comical, very;
Who has gone through the world, not mindful of pelf,
Upon easy terms, thank Heaven, with himself,
Along bypaths and in pleasant ways,
Caring as little for censure as praise;
Having some friends whom he loves dearly,
And no lack of foes, whom he laughs at sincerely;
And never for great, nor for little things,
Has he fretted his guts to fiddle-strings.
He might have made them by such folly
Most musical, most melancholy.

Sic cecinit Robertus, anno aetatis suæ 55.

Inscription for a Coffee Pot

A golden medal was voted to me
By a certain Royal Society:
'Twas not a thing at which to scoff,
For fifty guineas was the cost thereof:
On one side a head of the king you might see,
And on the other was Mercury!
But I was scant of worldly riches,
And moreover the Mercury had no breeches;
So, thinking of honour and utility too,

And having modesty also in view,
I sold this medal, (why should I not?)
And with the money which for it I got,
I purchased this silver coffee-pot:
Which I trust my son will preserve with care,
To be handed down from heir to heir.
These verses are engraven here,
That the truth of the matter may appear,
And I hope the society will be so wise,
As in future to dress their Mercuries!

[1830]

Index of First Lines

III